Book Map

Where can I take you?

Use this list to get directly to your IT area of interest.

Aligning Expectations

Attraction Strategy

Best Practices

Buy-in

Careers

Collaboration

IT MANAGEMENT FACTORS'

They are all interconnected

Politics

Teamwork Harmony

Business relationship management Collaboration

Partnering Vendor management

Expectations alignment Relationships

No surprises Communication Buy-in

Proactive competence Client focus Service quality

Creativity Best people

Effective information technology

Business case methodology Strategic integration

Strategic performance

Research Commercialization

Business results Innovation

Continuous improvement

Investment strategy Benchmarking

Continuous training Staff development

Best practices

Communication

Empowerment

Initiative

Innovation

No Surprises

Political Games

Research

Strategic Integration

Team Focus

Vendor Management

Praise for "Technical Impact"

"Al Kuebler's book, "Technical Impact" will help you keep IT relevant and make your career count. The book is brief and—perhaps as an illustration of its effectiveness—uses flowcharts and a 'book map.' The map allows you to jump right to the page that covers what you want to do at your company—say, commercialize an IT function."

— **CIO Magazine**

ଔଥଔ

"Al Kuebler shows IT managers at all levels how to communicate the benefits of IT in business terms. He also shows business leaders what they can expect from an effective IT management function. If you want to save money while growing your enterprise with IT, you'll want to get and use the knowledge in this book."

— **Bob Boor**
Chief Technology Officer
Royal Bank of Scotland Group

ଔଥଔ

"This tremendously useful guide illustrates how customer satisfaction and bottom-line results are enhanced through effective leveraging of the IT function. Al Kuebler provides a roadmap that fosters company-wide collaboration while empowering IT professionals to actively contribute to overall business strategy and leadership."

— **Abe Eshkenazi CSCP, CPA, CAE**
Chief Executive Officer, APICS
The Association for Operations Management

ೞ

"If you read only one chapter, make it, 'What Are You Doing for Me and Why Don't I Know It?' It's right on the money. As Kuebler puts it, our primary function in IT is to directly understand what the business does and needs and *communicate* what IT is doing for it."

— **Ray Crescenzi**
Senior Vice President, Technical Services
ABN AMRO

ೞ

"Al Kuebler makes a strong case for the importance of life-long learning, and then offers the reader a high-impact short course to becoming the IT business partner organizations need and the leader people deserve, as well as finding the route to a successful IT career. Here is the means to shorten your learning curve and drive top-level outcomes for you, your team and your business."

— **Gayle Magee**
Senior Faculty,
The Center for Creative Leadership

ೞ

"An easy-to-read, invaluable guide to highly effective strategic, proactive IT leadership. A critical tool for the career growth and development, and the career longevity, of IT managers and leaders."

— **Walter Polsky**
President
Cambridge Human Resource Group,
A leadership development and coaching firm

⊂3୫⊃

"Al Kuebler's priorities—partnership and involvement with those who need IT leadership—and his approach of delivering value through IT and keeping things simple and practical changed my approach to business. By following the principles that Al conveys, you will be better able to use IT for competitive advantage, and ROI will be much more directly achievable. His is advice that transcends industry specialty or professional discipline. The knowledge in this book will make your cost for IT ever more productive."

— **Preston W. Blevins**
CFPIM, FBPICS, CIRM, CSCP
Author of Food Safety Regulatory Compliance: Catalyst for a Lean and Sustainable Food Supply Chain

⊂3୫⊃

"Al Kuebler does a great job of demystifying IT for business owners like me who don't have a technical background. I recommend that entrepreneurs read this book to understand what they need from technology, and how to get it."

— **Todd Feldman**
Founder of PicJur,
a leading developer
of visual study aids for law schools

TECHNICAL IMPACT

MAKING YOUR INFORMATION TECHNOLOGY EFFECTIVE, AND KEEPING IT THAT WAY

AL KUEBLER

Make Your IT Career Last.
Make It Count.

International Standard Book Number (ISBN):

ISBN: 1-50055-578-9
ISBN/EAN13: 978-1-50055-578-8

First edition May 2010
Revised edition July 2010
Second edition January 2011
Third edition August 2012
Fourth edition July 2014

LIBRARY OF CONGRESS CATALOGING-IN-PUBLICATION DATA

Kuebler, Al

Technical impact: making your information technology
effective, and keeping it that way / Al Kuebler
Includes index.
LCCN: 2010903697
1. Business management. 2. Strategic performance.
3. Information technology.

Book Industry Standards and Communications (BISAC) Category:
Business & Economics/Information Management

Printed in the United States of America

To my dearest Jan,
with all my love and gratitude.

CONTENTS

Acknowledgments

I'm most grateful to my superb, always-focused-on-the-message and articulate editor of the last two years, Jamie Eckle, who unfailingly understood what I meant and tirelessly helped me clearly and concisely express it.

Thank you, Jamie. I couldn't have done this without you.

I'm also most grateful to those I've worked with in my career—whether I worked for them, they worked for me, or we worked alongside each other—who took the time to help me and the others around them develop and grow, or who simply inspired excellence with their own example. There are too many of you to name here, but you are the "Performers" (see Chapter 12) that we all feel lucky to find by our professional side. And, due to the close relationships we developed over the years (even after several successive employers), you know who you are.

Because of you, my professional journey was made ever better, right from the beginning. Thank you.

—Al Kuebler

About This Book

Each chapter of this book conveys one or more lessons about making IT effective. You can read the chapters in order, but I recommend that you just find a chapter on a topic you're particularly interested in and dive in to that, then go off and find another one.

I've done a few things to make that easier.

Each chapter has a subject heading on its title page. Of course, each chapter actually deals with multiple topics, and the book map inside the front cover arranges the chapters by additional topics. At the back of the book, a more traditional index is another guide.

So, go ahead and jump in.

Introduction

The purpose of this book is simply to provide you with four things:

- Proven ways to make the contribution of the IT function as beneficial as possible to the business it serves;
- Proven ways to ensure that the IT function is fully recognized for the positive impact it has on business performance;
- Enough explicit examples to instill confidence that these approaches are doable in any IT organization; and,
- Advice on how to get started, even though you have no buy-in except your own.

I've found that the collective use and adaptation of these lessons has an important outcome: *an IT function that is continuously improving its effectiveness to the enterprise.*

This book is intended for IT professionals and general managers who wish to make their IT management function more directly responsive to the businesses they serve.

It will also give IT professionals insight into ways to make their IT career last and make it count, remain enthusiastic about their contributions and improve their sense of accomplishment and reward.

They are lessons that I believe will be of value to you whether your IT career is at the starting gate or near the finish line.

In my case, the insights I share in these pages were hard won. I suppose it's possible that somewhere there exists a business school student so adept as to learn the inner workings of IT and corporate organizations before even entering the workforce. Some of us are lucky enough to learn from a mentor who takes a personal interest in our development. But most of us in this industry learn the hard way—through experience. My hope is that *my* experiences, transmitted through this book, will offer a short cut of sorts for you.

Most of the stories in the following chapters come from my nearly thirty years of observation and practice as a business and IT executive and as an IT management consultant. Some, though, were passed on to me by other managers, and still others came to me from thoughtful people who kindly took me aside and asked, "Have you ever thought about it this way?"

By the way, don't assume that what I have to tell you is irrelevant to your career because all my experiences happened more than ten minutes ago. This book is about how you can make what technology has to offer available to your business and so help it become more competitive and profitable. But what it talks about is how to go about using collaboration, communication and persuasion to do that. More than technology itself, it is about *people and relationships.* Unlike technology, those things don't change.

Some of these chapters have appeared as IT management articles in *CIO, Computerworld, InfoWorld* and other publications. To all of those who read those articles, recommended them to others or wrote to me in response to them, I should let you know that you got me going on my mission to get this book completed. I'm most grateful to you.

I heard an IT manager say once, "Each day it seems that there's more and more that I know less and less about. I hope I can retire before anyone finds out."

Understandable perhaps, but if you have *great relationships* alongside you, the journey can be wonderful.

—Al Kuebler

Being a Proactive Leader: The Value Proposition

> The idea that IT professionals don't need business acumen is a destructive myth.

L et me be very clear: To make a lasting and strategic impact on your enterprise or institution, you must be a proactive partner in realizing what its leaders wish to achieve.

The value of IT is under assault every day. You might chalk this up to business leaders who just don't get IT; that's what I used to think. But then I learned a much more productive approach, encapsulated in the IT value proposition illustration on the next page. I recommend it to any IT leader who wants a lasting career leading teams that make significant contributions to the performance of the business (while getting all of the recognition due them). Business leaders are not likely to get IT until you explain its value to them in ways they understand. Once you begin to do that, you will earn their respect. They will consider you a proactive partner and a powerful ally in achieving success for them and the enterprise.

THE IT VALUE PROPOSITION

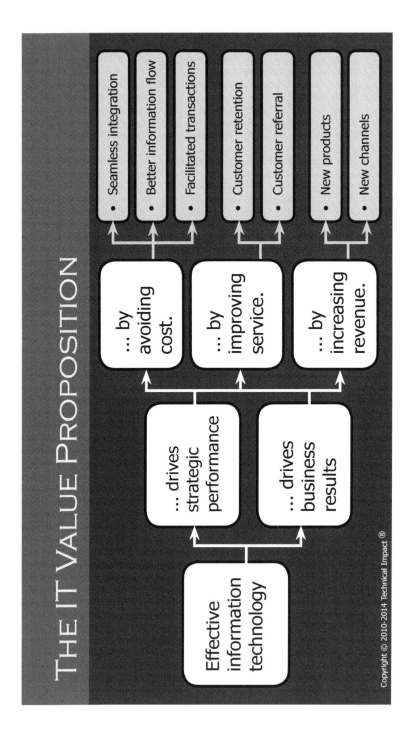

Effective information technology

... drives strategic performance

... drives business results

... by avoiding cost.

... by improving service.

... by increasing revenue.

- Seamless integration
- Better information flow
- Facilitated transactions
- Customer retention
- Customer referral
- New products
- New channels

In this book, I present many lessons from my career in information technology, but collectively, they are summarized in that opening paragraph. If you don't want to run the risk of being just another CIO whose initialism stands for "career is over," I strongly suggest that you take it to heart.

I know that many of you will protest that the attacks on the IT function simply aren't justified. Well, some of them are, though I agree that many of them are not. That isn't the point, really. I've seen well-intended and capable IT managers at all levels attacked for problems with business profitability and growth that were completely the responsibility of the business unit making the attack. When it happens, what matters is not whether the attack is justified; the important thing is how the IT manager addresses it. IT managers who believe that what they are doing is an isolated and reactive specialty and the only thing in the enterprise that is worthy of their focus are often caught off balance by such attacks. And they usually end up being replaced.

Relationships Are Everything

For the reactive IT manager, it's simply incomprehensible that anyone in the business leadership might not fully understand or appreciate what IT does. More often than not, this is why such managers spend so little time explaining to business peers what they're up to (and virtually no time finding out what their business peers are up to). In their minds, the necessity of what the IT function does is so obvious that it's inconceivable that it would ever have to be spelled out for anyone with the mental capacity to run a business unit.

The proactive IT manager, on the other hand, is better equipped to handle such an attack, because he or she has strong relationships that run deep throughout the enterprise that make it possible to understand the problem at its root and suggest ways that technology could help overcome it. More importantly, though, if the IT function is a proactive partner to the enterprise and every business in it, *it would be just plain silly to attack it.*

The proactive IT leader is keenly aware that the IT function will have value only if it benefits the enterprise and those benefits are clearly understood at all levels, both in the company and in the IT function itself. I like the phrase "part of it, proud of it" as a way to express how the proactive IT community relates to the business it serves.

Once these goals are understood, the principles and objectives necessary to achieve them almost suggest themselves. All the same, I will provide you with some guidelines to help you get on the right path.

- **Learn about the business your function serves, and get involved in making it better.**

If you believe that IT professionals don't need any particular insight into the nature of the business they serve, then you have bought into a destructive myth. IT leadership cannot remain isolated from the business it serves. A proactive leader seeks to understand as much as possible about how the enterprise acquires customers and makes money, strives to see its business performance goals from a shareholder perspective, uncovers the things restricting strategic achievement, and absorbs every part of the annual report. With that information, the IT leader can prepare a list of initiatives that the IT function could pursue to avoid cost, improve service and increase revenue.

- **Depend on others to define the value of your efforts.**

The proactive IT leader determines which business leaders can influence his or her success. Those people are IT's clients. You must meet with each of them and have wide-ranging discussions to find out what their goals are. Your value will be proportional to the degree to which you can help them achieve their success. Ask them how your IT function could make things better for them. Their answers will direct your team's efforts. And remember, this is not a one-time exercise. Repeat these meetings routinely; don't wait until there is a crisis.

• Build a creative IT organization.

Creative organizations are more flexible, move much faster and are much more competitive. That requires stripping away bureaucracy, so that decisions for action can be made at every level in the IT function. And it requires making it clear to your staff that when their initiatives lead to mistakes, their careers won't suffer. Your staff members need to feel safe and know there is little or no risk associated with being creative. (Allowing for risk-free mistakes is probably too radical, but do set an example by tolerating most mistakes, especially when initiative is involved.) In fact, a mistake made by a trusted and experienced employee who has taken initiative on behalf of a client can be invaluable if it is turned into a lesson that is openly shared. When no mistakes are made, then no creative initiatives are being undertaken, and that means no growth, or worse.

• Embrace change.

Astute IT management accepts that the IT function will adapt as the business and technology worlds around it change. But we all resist change, even though the most significant events in our careers are those that force us to change. And the more experienced we are, the more we fear to venture. However, it is essential to embrace the idea that change is not only anticipated (as it must be in the world of IT), but is also very beneficial to the enterprise. In fact, the IT function is a powerful business change agent. Most CEOs know this and expect their IT management to show them how the introduction of emerging technologies and new approaches can accelerate and improve their strategic business performance. Business general managers increasingly look to IT to introduce change through beneficial ideas that arise because of IT's unique perception of the entire enterprise. I can guarantee you that change will happen anyway; you might as well lead it, help it along and target it.

- **Measure quality in IT services.**

This is one of the most critical factors in making IT a proactive partner to the business. You are not going to get blind acceptance of what IT is doing, and acting as if you should is a *career-limiting move* for any CIO. Measuring IT quality involves jointly setting service-level standards, providing recognition for joint accomplishment, showing the enterprise that the IT function is not resting in terms of its performance and productivity, leading the way in continuous improvement, and much more. Doing all of this has become easier as IT best practices have matured. The payoffs are improved IT productivity and the endorsement you will get from your business peers.

- **Hire the best people, and hold on to them.**

You can't have a creative IT organization without the best

people. It's a lot of work sorting out the best and finding ways to attract them and keep them, but it's worth it. The surest way to outperform the competition is to have better people than them. And of course, we all know that outcomes don't turn out the way we planned them. But if we have the best people and they are properly organized and motivated, they will be able to deal with the unexpected things that are sure to come.

• Benchmark the IT function.

This lets you show how your internal IT function outperforms other commercial offerings available to the company, at a lower cost. And if a non-strategic service can be done cheaper, faster and better by an external provider, you have an obligation to the stockholders to suggest moving to it. It's also important to realize that benchmarking can pinpoint areas that need attention. Just be aware that benchmarking by itself can lead to mediocrity. Getting your IT services to the point where they are considered "commercial grade" is just your starting point for continuous improvement. Take this seriously, or your stockholders will soon have the burden of paying the profit margin of an outside commercial IT service provider. And with the IT function farmed out, there won't be much left for a CIO to do.

• Know your numbers.

You have to be prepared to answer questions such as: "What percentage of the enterprise's total revenue is your IT budget?" "What is the annual rate of change for the IT budget?" "How much has the IT function's productivity improved over the last three years?" "How has the IT function helped the enterprise avoid cost, improve service or increase revenue?

By how much?" "Why should a stockholder want to give any CIO any increase at all?" "How much would the company spend if it outsourced the entire IT function?" "Does the IT function deliver useful information to the business, and how does that quantifiably help the company's competitive position, in terms of profit?" If you don't have answers, no worries; you'll get them. Or else.

- **Have a clue about what the IT future holds.**

As an IT leader, it is part of your job to keep an eye on what is going to be coming in the technology sphere and introducing your enterprise to the ways it could benefit from it. If you are not aware of what is going on, you risk proposing investments in technology at the end of its technical life, and at much too high a price. When you do your research homework properly, you will know when a new technology has reached the maturity your organization needs before it becomes overpriced because of demand. The senior management committee will appreciate your research and forethought as you provide carefully considered advice on acquiring the IT capacity the company needs.

- **You want your IT function to work together as a team, so be a good team member yourself.**

The first step is to realize that your behavior will clearly signal whether or not you are a supportive member of your team. This will be noticed. Meet regularly at all levels with parts of your IT organization, in small enough groups so that you can know their names and functions and have one-to-one exchanges to better understand the challenges they face. It's wise to remember when you were in similar positions and to ask things such as "What do you need to be more productive?" Every second of these meetings, you'll be carefully observed for authentic team member behavior. Listen to your team members' concerns and questions, and keep in mind that if someone bothered to ask you about something, then he or she has the expectation that you might actually do something about it. Therefore, if possible, you must, and if you can't, then you need to explain why truthfully. Take notes so that you can follow up with appropriate actions when you can. If training is needed, fund it. If better equipment is needed, arrange for it when you can.

In all of this, your visibility and responsiveness will send the message that you will do all you can to enable your team to perform more effectively. And, when you bother to find out what your team members want for their careers and give them tasks and training that help them get there, you generate energy, enthusiasm and excitement. Pay attention to individuals so you'll know who has potential, and then give them tasks that will make them stretch; never forget how good you felt when that was done for you. Your contribution to teamwork also requires you to set clear and unambiguous goals and to provide information freely so that the team knows where they stand regarding *their* progress in achieving them. When team members feel that they are believed in, trusted and know where they stand, they will help each other to jointly achieve their common goals. Your outcome will be an IT function with increased focus on results and an ever-increasing momentum toward their attainment.

- ### Don't look back.

What you design and produce today with care and love will be completely dismantled and rebuilt by your successors. Savor your successes, but keep them in the past. Keep your focus on moving your team forward to their next worthy achievement.

❁

Did I say all this would be easy? I hope not.

But if you think that something from the list above will be particularly difficult for you because it just isn't one of your strengths, well, recognizing your weaknesses is itself a strength. The way you deal with that is to identify someone who has the strength you lack and ask that person to join your team. There is absolutely no need to be shy about that sort of thing. Every person I have ever approached in this way has appreciated the recognition, and working together only magnified the rapport we had. And don't forget, building rapport both within your team and among your peers is one of the main tasks of the proactive IT leader.

Each chapter that follows is a story from my career. I hope the lessons they impart are as useful to you as they were for me in my career. As a philosopher once said, "I'm glad you are here. I'm glad I'm here. I believe I have something valuable to share with you."

CHAPTER 2

What Are You Doing for Me, and Why Don't I Know It?

> Without a formal communication plan, you could find your IT function being outsourced from under you.

I was invited to an urgent, one-on-one meeting with the CIO of a very large IT organization. No hint of the subject matter. Upon arrival, I saw that he was very disturbed about something, but he simply handed me a copy of an e-mail he had recently received from the chairman of the board:

> There is such widespread dissatisfaction with data processing within the company that I think we need an outside consultant to come in and determine how and what we can outsource or how we should organize ourselves. The costs are going up with the tight labor market, and as I suspected when we raised our IT salaries, performance doesn't seem to have improved in the eyes of the users. In fact, I believe it is getting worse.
>
> You and I have such a different idea of how well we are doing than the users that I can't see any other

way to put the train back on the track.

I don't want another survey like the one we just had; that is too depressing. But we need to see how we can get at least some of our users believing that they are getting value for money. I would bet at this point that we wouldn't win one vote if we put ourselves up for election.

Any ideas or any suggestions on what consulting group to use? A general management firm or a more DP-oriented group?

After I reread the e-mail a couple of times, the CIO talked at length about the many unplanned challenges his organization had met over the past seven years and the many initiatives that had been launched to improve the responsiveness and cost-effectiveness of almost every aspect of IT services. He explained that his organization had successfully absorbed seven acquisitions with no interruptions to existing application systems and services. He told me about the very high numbers of transactions that were successfully handled on a daily and yearly basis. He also explained his practice of meeting with the end users of his services to glean their perceptions about IT. He did all this and more, thoroughly convincing me that users' complaints were off the mark.

Then he asked, "What can I do about this?"

"You can ask the chairman for a ninety-day delay before he pursues outsourcing any further," I said.

"What," he wanted to know, "can we possibly hope to accomplish in ninety days?"

"A lot."

Communication Is Not a Four-letter Word

I suspected that the general managers of the business groups were unaware of the things that the CIO had just told me about. These accomplishments in all probability had never been communicated to the business groups, at least not in the business terms they understood.

We often fail to make an effort to communicate our accomplishments because we think they are obvious enough that everyone will see them. But business managers don't know what we know about IT. What they know about IT is that it's very expensive, and they suspect that they aren't getting their money's worth.

Certainly, this CIO wasn't blind to the need to communicate. He had met with users at lower management levels in an effort to find out about their perceptions of IT. His mistake was to think that what those users told him was the same thing they told the general managers. In business, lower-level managers are notorious for telling those above them whatever they want to hear. And from what the chairman had said in his e-mail, the general managers clearly didn't appreciate the value of the IT function.

The CIO got his extension, and we set out on a plan to help general management appreciate the strategic and operational business value that the IT function contributed now, what it had contributed in the near past and what it would contribute in the future. A related goal was to let every IT professional know that they should take pride in these contributions and in their own place in what IT consistently does in support of the enterprise.

His response: "I've been trying to do that for years. How can it be done in ninety days?"

I explained that he needed to build a formal communication plan to stay in touch with clients and staff. It was obvious that this IT organization had done some very important things in support of the business. What it hadn't done was let the interested parties know.

YOUR IT TEAM'S EFFORTS MATTER, SO CONNECT

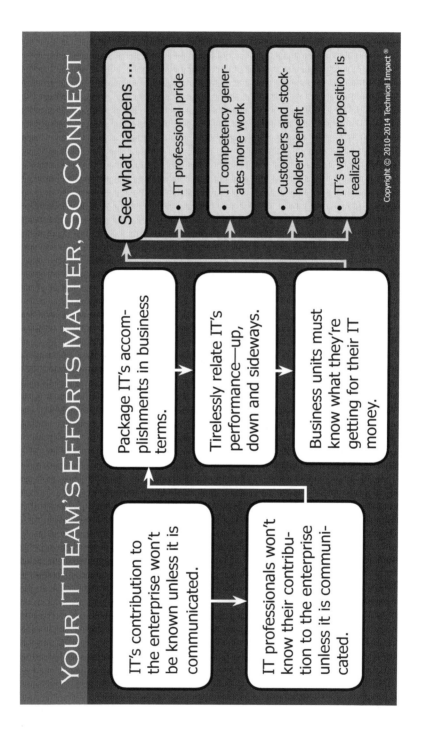

IT's contribution to the enterprise won't be known unless it is communicated.

IT professionals won't know their contribution to the enterprise unless it is communicated.

Package IT's accomplishments in business terms.

Tirelessly relate IT's performance—up, down and sideways.

Business units must know what they're getting for their IT money.

See what happens ...

- IT professional pride
- IT competency generates more work
- Customers and stockholders benefit
- IT's value proposition is realized

Over the next sixty days, we prepared a "yesterday, today and tomorrow" presentation that substantiated and broadened the message the CIO had conveyed to me in our conversation, putting it all in business terms. In it, the CIO explained that his department was changing its culture from a focus on technology to one on business processes, that it was very involved in all business activities, that it clearly understood that business drives technology, that it had remained responsive to business changes in spite of dramatic growth through many acquisitions, and that it had added business value.

He also demonstrated that his organization was doing all this less expensively than could be done by any alternatives.

The CIO's very credible and understandable theme was simply that his technology function is much more than an expense. It is also a cost-effective, powerful ally and a partner involved in almost every aspect of the enterprise.

So, what happened?

During the final thirty days of the chairman's grace period, the CIO repeatedly gave this presentation to the general management of the enterprise, including the chairman, and to all levels within his IT organization. It was so well received that he was requested to give it nine more times in the following six weeks.

The chairman shelved the notion of outsourcing the IT function.

Going Beyond First Steps

Of course, the only way to keep dissatisfaction at bay is to keep such presentations updated and give them annually at a minimum.

To his credit, the CIO wasn't finished just yet. Slowly, within the CIO's own organization, the understanding that what IT did avoided cost, improved service or increased revenue resulted in a small but growing sense of pride. And to ensure that he would never repeat such a lapse in communication, the CIO established a small business relationship management (BRM) function as part of his IT organization but outside of the usual plan, build and run technology parts. This new function reports directly to him.

Further, he engaged outside consulting help proficient in BRM transformation processes to more fully develop the interpersonal and communication skills of his BRM unit and IT professional staff. Among many other key communication and commercialization initiatives, this BRM function has since maintained the CIO's presentation as current. He continues to give it every year.

At some point during the information-gathering process, I had mentioned an ancient Chinese saying to the CIO: "You tell me, and I forget. You show me, and I remember. You *involve* me, and I understand." He looked at me and said, "Got it!"

CHAPTER 3

Reactive Bystander, or Proactive Partner?

> *You can't help your clients achieve their objectives if you don't know what they are.*

Business leaders' complaints about IT haven't changed much over the years. IT people speak their own jargon. They don't understand what stockholders and business leaders value. They're isolated from the business. They focus on technology at the cost of everything else.

Pressed, they might say that things have gotten better over the years. But I guarantee there are very few of them who see IT as an equal partner in the pursuit of goals that can be summed up in just six words: *avoid cost; improve service; increase revenue.*

Sure, at some level, every IT professional realizes that what IT does serves a business purpose, but that awareness is fairly dim for most of us (this once included me, by the way). After all, most of us went into this field because it was technology that interested us. Business in and of itself? Not so much.

Can we really change the perceptions of IT among business leaders? Sure, if we change our approach to them and learn to address the topic of technology's intersection with business in the language they understand. Consider the following two scenarios in which an IT guy meets with a business manager. The first is fairly typical of what happens all the time in businesses around the country. The second is somewhat idealized but illustrates an approach that we all can learn to use.

Act I, Scene 1

IT GUY, *entering the office of a business manager:* I heard that you wanted to see me. How can I help you?

BUSINESS MANAGER: You can tell me why I shouldn't get my IT support from someone who's cheaper. I'm not in the business of seeing my profit margins shrink while you IT guys add all the technology toys you want. Message clear?

IT GUY: It sure is. I'll get back to you promptly on this.

Act I, Scene 2

One week later.

BUSINESS MANAGER: Okay, what have you got for me?

IT GUY, *handing over some papers:* I've been looking at the PC and help desk support we provide your business, and our benchmarks, which you can verify, show that our costs are less than you'd pay if you decided to outsource it.

BUSINESS MANAGER, *unhappy:* Boy, oh boy, I get to verify these numbers? You've got to be kidding me—is this what we're having this meeting for? Your hands are tied and there's nothing you can do about my cost issue?

IT GUY: Uh, sorry, I should have related the following first. I've analyzed your support situation and discovered that your business needs different levels of PC and help desk support based on the type of work that is done by your employees.

See? Your operations staff needs the current 24/7 PC and help desk support, with half-hour on-site assistance, but most managerial and administrative staffs need only ten hours of support five days a week, with a two-hour, on-site assistance expectation.

BUSINESS MANAGER, *a little interested:* So, where's all this leading?

IT GUY: Well, I can't reduce your costs for your operations staff unless you tell me that you're okay with less support— either fewer days per week, fewer hours per day or a longer on-site assistance expectation.

BUSINESS MANAGER: Well, I'm sure that my operations people need the current level of IT support, but now that you've posed the question, I'll see if I can reduce some cost there without adding too much risk. Is that all you've got?

IT GUY: No. Since about a third of your employees are in the managerial administrative support category, the capacity I need to support them is considerably less than for your 24/7 operational people. If you can wait six weeks for me to adjust things, my monthly charges to you can be less for this number of your employees by this amount.

BUSINESS MANAGER: Six weeks? I want you to get on this

right away. I'm sure you're busy, but every day less than six weeks helps our stockholders. I appreciate what you've done here, but from now on I want to hear suggestions from you before I have to ask. Understood?

IT GUY: Understood.

⁂

Act II, Scene 1

Newly hired IT guy has called for an introductory meeting with the business manager.

IT GUY: I'm glad you had time to fit me in. I didn't come to steal your time, only to introduce myself and let you know that I'm just a phone call away for any issues that you might have with the support we provide you and your people.

BUSINESS MANAGER: Well, I wasn't prepared to discuss issues today, but if I have any, I'll certainly let you know.

IT GUY: I would appreciate that. And please, call me Walt.

BUSINESS MANAGER: Okay, Walt. I'm Sam.

WALT: Before I go, Sam, I'd like you to know that sometime when you have a chance, I'd very much like to understand your business processes and the role IT plays in it, from your perspective.

SAM: What do you mean?

WALT: Well, your customer acquisition cycle, your customer service/retention cycle, what pull-through your business provides or receives from other parts of the enterprise—all that would be of interest. Your short- and long-term goals would also be of value to me, when you have the time. If I understood your situation better, I could perhaps suggest some ways for you to avoid cost while improving service and maybe even increasing revenue.

Sam is intrigued and uses his whiteboard to lay out his business and the role he sees IT playing in it. Meanwhile, Walt is alert, takes notes and makes drawings. He's not play-acting. He wants to remember what he's being told so he can later come up with a course of action.

WALT, *taking his leave:* I very much appreciate your taking time to share all of this with me. This has been extremely helpful. If you don't mind, I'd like to arrange another meeting with you shortly so we can go over all this and make sure I've gotten it all right. At that time, I'd like to share any potential opportunities that I see for better dealing with the issues you've raised, as well as avoiding cost, improving service and increasing revenue. I may even be able to suggest some ways to deal with some short-term headaches, but it's too early to promise anything. I have to learn more on my end. Anyway, I'm certain that an ongoing dialogue could be very productive. In the meantime, Sam, if something occurs to you that needs my attention, I'd be grateful if you'd personally let me know right away.

SAM: Okay, Walt. I won't forget.

❖

The difference?

In the first example, the IT guy really thinks he's being

GREAT IT RELATIONSHIPS START WITH INITIATIVE

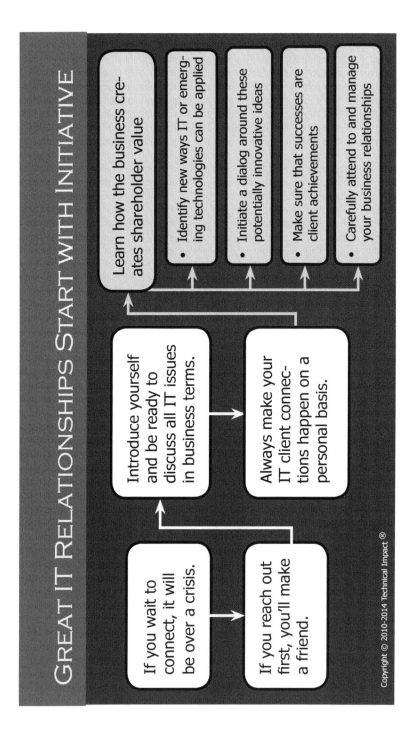

If you wait to connect, it will be over a crisis.

If you reach out first, you'll make a friend.

Introduce yourself and be ready to discuss all IT issues in business terms.

Always make your IT client connections happen on a personal basis.

Learn how the business creates shareholder value

- Identify new ways IT or emerging technologies can be applied
- Initiate a dialog around these potentially innovative ideas
- Make sure that successes are client achievements
- Carefully attend to and manage your business relationships

helpful and responsive. But he's only being reactive. The business manager feels as if he has to wring information about avoiding costs out of him.

In the second scenario, the entire session was directed by Walt, who seemed to promise more involvement in Sam's domain than Sam had ever expected from any IT professional. What's more, Walt seemed to understand most of the business issues that Sam discussed.

Walt didn't come to Sam with his hat in his hand. He had enough confidence to know that IT could be a powerful ally and an involved partner to business needs, and he didn't wait to be asked. He proactively pressed to find out what his client's needs were and to help surface specific areas where he could help. By the way, I've seen it done the other way, where the business manager is the new guy. Once again, it's the IT guy who takes the initiative, visiting the new business manager within a few weeks of his arrival.

Of course, Walt's interpersonal skills and business-oriented language are acquired capabilities for most of us. Some coaching from those proficient in these types of consultative and business skills will usually be needed to raise our levels (Ouellette & Associates is a firm I've used often that specializes in this type of IT communication skills coaching). An ongoing client relationship management program can be helpful in maintaining and further developing these skills over time.

The really good news is that this kind of transformation always results in the company's increased appreciation for the IT community. That causes a corresponding energy release within the IT community, making it even more responsive to the enterprise.

All this comes about when IT professionals proactively communicate with their clients in simple business terms to understand their linked destiny. When this happens, the IT community can no longer be a reactive bystander to what goes on in the business. Successfully achieving the company's strategy becomes the jointly shared outcome that stockholders have every right to expect.

CHAPTER 4

What My Clients Taught Me

> *It's a long list, but it can all be boiled down to a single sentence.*

I was very fortunate very early in my career to learn that all anyone really needs to know about meeting clients' expectations.

It's very simple really, because all that's necessary is to treat our clients the way we would want to be treated when we do business with a commercial service provider.

As I said, simple. But sometimes there's nothing harder than giving credence to a really simple idea. As IT professionals, we know how truly complicated things can be. At the time of my great lesson, I had been up to my neck in a project to rationalize the distributed systems of a large corporation. This company had made roughly two acquisitions every year for the previous six years. Its distributed systems were in chaos, since each acquired company had its own distributed systems and software. (Architecture? Be serious!) Documents or files created in one business couldn't be opened or used in another business or at the corporate level.

It was anything but simple.

We eventually hammered things into shape. Help desk calls went down. Documents could be sent and received and actually used. E-mails were proactively screened for viruses. Productivity went up. Businesses could collaborate better and faster, and the total cost of ownership of distributed systems technology and support went down significantly.

Having accomplished so much, I decided to find out what our clients thought of it all. I dislike survey forms, so I decided to do a personal survey, taking notes as I talked to each client. I got the questions down to three, set up an interview schedule with business managers, corporate officers and general management, and began in earnest.

My three questions were:

1. What concerns do you have with the IT services that you receive?
2. How would you characterize the IT support function that provides IT services to you today?
3. What would you desire in your IT services in the future?

The first two questions were aimed at identifying specific short-term improvements, while Question 3 was intended to confirm these improvements as outcomes. More importantly, responses to Question 3 would give me insight into what clients saw as the most valued performance characteristics of any IT service provider.

After about twenty interviews, a pattern began to emerge. After fifty-seven interviews, the pattern became so locked in that I've never had to do a survey again.

The responses to Questions 1 and 2 led me to implement

YOUR LAST IT SERVICES CLIENT SURVEY

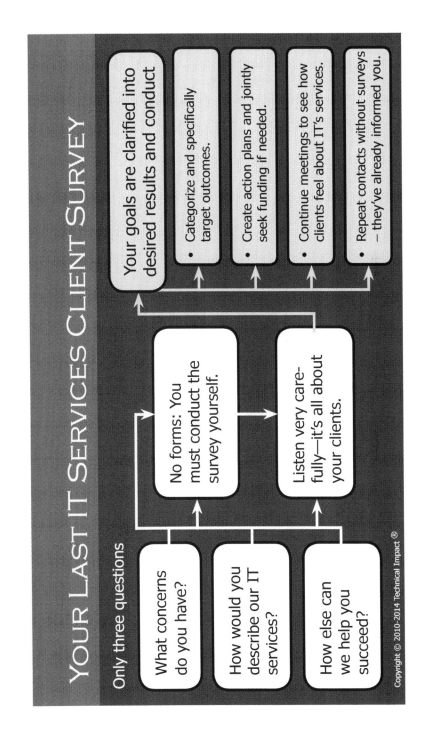

Only three questions

What concerns do you have?

How would you describe our IT services?

How else can we help you succeed?

No forms: You must conduct the survey yourself.

Listen very carefully—it's all about your clients.

Your goals are clarified into desired results and conduct

- Categorize and specifically target outcomes.
- Create action plans and jointly seek funding if needed.
- Continue meetings to see how clients feel about IT's services.
- Repeat contacts without surveys – they've already informed you.

IT management best practices and to improve the interpersonal and consultative skills of my staff. As a result, my staff became more focused on the client experience and on helping each other instead of being focused on ensuring that everyone's backside was covered.

But it was the responses to Question 3 that made the simplicity of it all blindingly clear. My clients' desired outcomes were in fact the same as mine for any service I receive. They wanted the experience to be quick, easy, accurate and pleasant. But I began to hear something else in their responses. In my clients' own words, here's what they expressed to me:

In terms of performance conduct, I want my IT service provider to be:

- Proactive with regard to my needs.
- A provider of exclusive services, if needed.
- The best engineering provider.
- An innovative partner and ally to the business.
- Committed to me.
- An exceptional performer.
- The best technology supplier.
- Responsive, informative, confident and creative.
- Price-competitive and predictable.
- Easy to buy from.

In terms of service results, I want my IT service provider to:

- Understand my needs.
- Deliver as promised.
- Speak in my terms.
- Alleviate my concerns and risks.
- Guarantee my satisfaction.

- Demonstrate sustained improvements.
- Lead me to better ways.
- Help me succeed.

In the many IT assignments I've had since that one, these IT service outcomes have stood the test of time. In fact I've never seen a circumstance where they don't apply.

In keeping with the idea that the principle behind all of the specific IT service outcomes I discovered in my last survey is simple, let me offer this very short quote by Napoleon Hill: "It is literally true that you can succeed best by helping others to succeed."

CHAPTER 5

Four Practical Practices

> *Easy ways to help you stay focused on the management principles you value.*

Not everything that I once thought was worthy of becoming a routine or practice proved useful. I either put them aside or kept changing and adding to them. What I ended up with can be summarized in four IT management practices that I can safely designate as good enough to stand the test of time. Together, these four guidelines did the following for me:

- Helped keep my focus on improving and developing my team, and,
- Ensured that strategic matters remained a consistent priority whenever practicable.

In other words, these practices served as consistent, practical (not theoretical) reminders to make me stay connected to the things I valued most as an IT manager. You can adapt and refine them as needed for your situation, but I believe that they can be applied in some form to any management level of the IT function.

• How will your IT services be perceived next year?

This question became my guide when I realized that the trio of questions that I had been asking myself—"Where are we now? Where do we want to be? What's our course of action to get there?"—were not specific enough and couldn't be easily related to collective outcomes. Eventually, I prepared for the upcoming year by asking my team whether they thought our department and our IT services would be perceived as:

- A knowledgeable partner with extensive capabilities.
- An integrated part of the business.
- A provider of excellent service.
- A partner with predictable and competitive pricing.
- Useful and helpful.
- The "safe" approach.
- The leader in effective IT application.
- A sloppy bureaucracy.
- Overpriced.
- A place with innovative people.
- A function that was not growing or improving.
- One that was getting worse.
- First in performance achievement against all alternatives.
- Ever better in price/performance.

With both positives and negatives on the list, the issues for the team became: (a) how do we make sure we don't get perceived as the negatives? and (b) what to we have to do to achieve the positives? The answers, naturally, were things like using benchmarking, undertaking interpersonal skill training, finding ways to improve client experience, implementing quality metrics and undergoing continuous improvement. I didn't find it daunting that achieving some of the positive client-focused outcomes might require a long and arduous process; the key factor was that the process would have begun. More importantly, it would be a jointly supported undertaking.

• Look back, but not in anger.

I like the George Santayana quote, "We must welcome the future, remembering that soon it will be the past; and we must respect the past, remembering that it was once all that was humanly possible." It gave me the idea that we needed to collectively appreciate our past accomplishments as a team, along with the vague notion that doing so would help us build upon those accomplishments. For a while, I didn't know what to do about this notion, but I ultimately hit on something that was utterly simple and very effective.

At the end of each year, my staff and I crafted a short memo to the entire department, called "Looking back for a moment." It recapped the happenings of the last twelve months, with an emphasis on team challenges that were overcome and team successes that improved our recognized value to the business. We included quotes from clients praising an IT area's performance—occasionally we even had some appreciative comments from the CEO or chairman to pass along. We were exhaustive about this, on the theory that the sheer volume of the praise sent a message to the team; I remember times when we had so many kudos we had to put them in an attachment.

The summaries of our challenges and accomplishments were broken down by team, followed by a list of every contributing team member. This recap set the stage for us to broadly indicate what we would need to address in the coming year, and if what loomed ahead seemed even more challenging than what we had already faced, the overall picture of competence and collaboration suggested that we were all up to meeting those new challenges.

The value of recognizing team achievements is all too often overlooked. Believe me, that memo was a great way of instilling confidence and pride in all of the team members. One time, I recall, I was walking behind a network specialist who was intently reading the just-issued memo, and I could hear him say, almost under his breath, "They actually noticed." Our year-end memo was one way of sending out that message of appreciation, but any method will work wonders.

- **Outperform politics.**

Inevitably, some members of your team will crave being in the limelight more than making a valuable contribution to your team's achievements. And at least once in your career, you will report to someone of this same type, whose leadership style is to use intimidation and control. I discuss both of these situations more in Chapter 12, but for now, be aware that your team is not safe when it has such members; you need to correct their behavior or remove them. If you do nothing, your team's energy, focus and momentum will be stolen, and your team's performance will be undermined. As for intimidating, credit-hogging managers, your weapon

STAY CLOSE TO YOUR STRATEGY AND YOUR TEAM

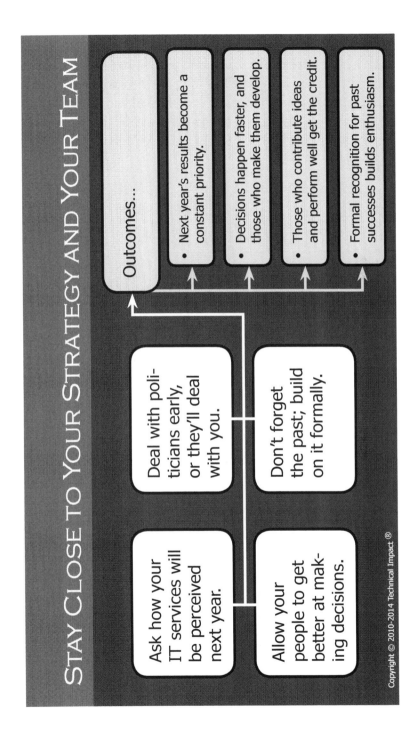

Ask how your IT services will be perceived next year.

Deal with politicians early, or they'll deal with you.

Allow your people to get better at making decisions.

Don't forget the past; build on it formally.

Outcomes...

- Next year's results become a constant priority.

- Decisions happen faster, and those who make them develop.

- Those who contribute ideas and perform well get the credit.

- Formal recognition for past successes builds enthusiasm.

is formality, deployed in exacting memos that spell out precisely what you understand to be your team's assignments. Do this rigorously and you and your team will be left alone to concentrate on achievement. Politics is a game of sorts, one in which it is possible to outcompete and outperform.

- **Don't try to control everything.**

Early in my career, I thought that it was important that I give my all to every document that required my signature and every memo that needed my input. As time went by, I realized that this urge to control everything led to me getting more and more documents and memos to review, and the time I needed for strategic matters was being eaten up. That's why, whenever anything came my way, I started asking myself, "Why am I looking at this?" I came to see that because of my taking responsibility for everything, my department was becoming glacially bureaucratic. I was also depriving my staff of opportunities to make decisions. People don't get better at making decisions if they don't have to make any.

What's more, I didn't know enough about many of the issues that were presented to me, and so I had to spend a lot of time sorting them out. I had hired people who did know about these things, but I was holding them back by acting like a hovering micromanager.

Eventually, I changed all signature authorizations so that actions could be taken at the lowest practical level in the organization. At first, some of my staff were uncomfortable with taking on more responsibility, but that was my fault for letting them think for so long that they needn't take any. Some of my IT managers would bring me an issue and then ask me, "Don't you even want to see it?" No, I'd say, adding that the time had come for them to own the outcomes of their actions. I reasoned that it was my job to move folks out of their comfort zones so that they could learn.

Now, when a problem presented itself and I was asked, "What do you want us to do about it?" I would say something like, "You have a better understanding of the situation than I do. So, I want you to lay the problem out for me as briefly as possible, tell me what options you see, and give me *your* best proposal for effectively handling it."

Of course, I remained active in shaping some actions. And some mistakes were made, but we learned from them, and mistakes over time became ever more rare. As team members learned to take ownership for their decisions, they prepared their reasoning carefully. The fact that I could be more effective on strategic matters completely outweighed the tactical hiccup or two that occurred during the implementation of this practice.

I once heard Jim Vance say, "If you know what all of your people are doing, you are dying. If you don't, you're scared to death, but your team is succeeding and so are you." An oversimplification, I know, but he makes the point. And once you know that your team will do the right thing when you aren't around, it isn't scary at all.

VENDOR MANAGEMENT

CHAPTER 6

'Just Nuke 'em'

> *Or is there a better way to deal with vendors?*

I think that old line "You can't live with them, but you can't live without them" is really about IT vendors. We all need them, and these days IT seems more reliant on vendors than ever before, not just for equipment, but also for IT development, services and support.

But from my earliest days as an IT manager, my relations with vendors were difficult and reactive, and I don't think that is unusual. My seniors took a hard-nosed approach. "Don't worry about the contract," they'd say. "If they don't perform, just nuke 'em and swap them out." Or maybe the equally tough, "Just hold their feet to the fire. That never fails to bring 'em around."

Nuking vendors didn't seem like the best approach to me, not least of all because of the legal complications that I foresaw as a result of actually carrying out such a plan. Instead, I was trusting. If a vendor's representatives told me they would deliver a service or product at a certain time for a certain price, I took him at his word and moved on to address other duties.

If you've ever dealt with IT vendors, you probably know just how naïve this approach was. Inevitably, some agreement wasn't quite met. Vendors that were late or whose service was below the level agreed upon were ready with lots of excuses. I heard account service managers cite snow days and other natural phenomena as reasons for failing to perform as required. "We thought you knew what we were doing all along," one told me once, leaving me to think, "Actually, I thought *you* knew what you were doing, but I guess I was wrong." All of my attempts to move my complaints up the vendor hierarchy were short-circuited by unanswered phone calls and e-mails. Meanwhile, the vendor's account service managers would sympathize with me. They seemed to earn their keep by acting as heat shields for the higher-ups. I was getting nothing but empty promises.

I still didn't want to nuke the vendors—although a tactical strike against them did tempt me from time to time—but it was clear to me that my approach would have career-limiting consequences. If I didn't come up with a better way to achieve consistent and cost-effective results from vendors, my credibility as an IT manager would steadily decline. I obviously didn't have my vendors' attention, so I decided that they needed some of mine.

Escalation

The vendor that finally sent me over the edge had been contracted to send us many workstations for a call center. They arrived just before the weekend, giving us time to set them up and have them ready for Monday business. But we quickly discovered that all the machines were incorrectly configured.

It being the weekend, we could get no hands-on help from the vendor, so the local IT team set up a makeshift workbench and installed what was needed and put the equipment in place just minutes before the call center opened on Monday morning. What should have been a one-day, three-shift conversion took two days and six shifts.

Unhappy with the extra expense, I checked the specifications in our order. They were correct, and what we had received didn't match them. Talking with my on-site project manager, I had to concede that I had shown poor forethought in some aspects of the contract. Delivery was made too close to our go-live date, and the intervening weekend reduced vendor support to some telephone calls. We should have built enough time in the schedule to allow for recovery in the event of a problem and to accommodate an operational readiness test on each piece of equipment. That would also have permitted a go/no go decision point, so that we could have rescheduled the rollout and not risk business disruption. But we both knew that the root problem was that we could not trust our supplier. I made an appointment at the vendor's headquarters and, seeking justice, got on an airplane.

The executives at the meeting were conciliatory, but I became even more enraged when they told me that my order had gotten less attention than it perhaps deserved because they had received an order from a larger customer. Were they saying that our formal agreement need not be honored because a chance to make more profit had arisen? I felt as if *they* were nuking *me*.

Faced with my dismay, much flapping resulted. No, no, they assured me, they had misspoken. How could they make it good? I told them that I wanted them to cover our expenses that resulted from their lack of quality control. And I wanted on-site technical support and rapid access to spares for any deployments in the future. They quickly agreed.

As I was about to head back to the airport, the executives mentioned that my selection of their company as a supplier had been a good one. After all, because we had relied on them so often, my staff had been able to rectify the configuration problem on their own, and that was a sign of strength in our relationship. "It has taken us a while working together to get to this point, but your staff really knows our product, almost as well as we do."

I wasn't sure if I was supposed to take comfort in this, and pondered just what they were telling me all the way to the airport. Only after take-off did it hit me. Their real message was that a change in equipment suppliers would carry a significant cost for my company. In fact, my senior management and my company's shareholders probably wouldn't like such a decision very much. Was I a captive client to this supplier? I needed another vendor relationship management strategy. This one wasn't working.

Vendor Relationship Management 101

At this point, it became obvious to me that the problem was that we weren't dealing with our IT vendors professionally. Oh, we were all professionals, and we behaved professionally. But my people were proficient in their various areas of IT expertise; they were not expert at procuring services and designing contracts.

We used the total cost of ownership (TCO) methodology for selecting and acquiring all services, software and equipment suppliers, but we weren't strategically very good at it, despite having undergone training. It wasn't possible for my people to gain enough experience with this type of analysis to do it really well. The depth of analysis varied from manager to manager, dependent on the amount of time available to them and the product or service being assessed. And an important factor was that my staff's performance wasn't measured on the quality of their vendor selection outcomes.

What we needed was a group of professionals who were dedicated to the task of contracting with vendors and working with them full time. They would not be distracted by other duties, and their performance would be judged entirely on their ability to achieve success in our vendor relations. In short, I needed a dedicated IT vendor relationship management (VRM) unit employing professionals adept at devising technical contracts, analyzing TCO and evaluating vendor performance.

I went to the senior executive committee with a compelling business case (the examples of contracts gone awry were embarrassingly abundant), got funding and established my first IT VRM unit. It paid for itself many times over in its first year.

From that time, as I moved to other IT management positions, I was never without an IT VRM unit whose only assignment was to ensure that we were achieving the lowest TCO practicable with all of our hardware and software vendors. "Practicable" is a key word. Pricing in isolation can be misleading. The IT VRM unit deepened the TCO analyses significantly beyond what any IT technical manager could even consider. Among the things that the unit evaluated and verified were competitive offerings and their features, actual warranty/guarantee value, support qualifications, references, contracts or agreements with other entities that might have a conflict of interest, confidentiality, actual support responsiveness, time to ship, involvement in new product design, access to laboratory results, upgrades, beta testing participation and results evaluation, product life expectancy, compliance with industry standards and best practices, company fi-

VENDOR RELATIONSHIP MANAGEMENT 101

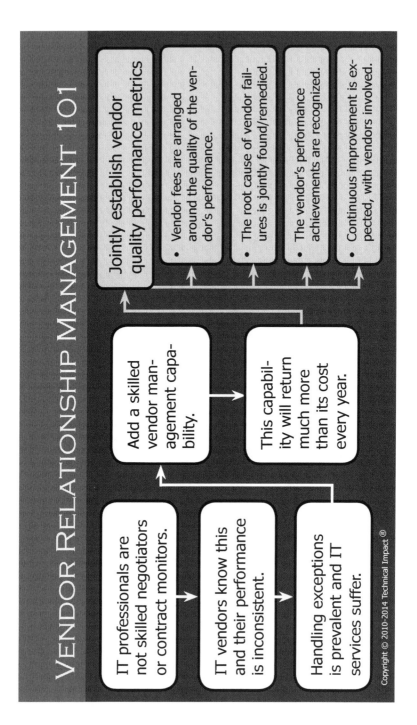

IT professionals are not skilled negotiators or contract monitors.

IT vendors know this and their performance is inconsistent.

Handling exceptions is prevalent and IT services suffer.

Add a skilled vendor management capability.

This capability will return much more than its cost every year.

Jointly establish vendor quality performance metrics

- Vendor fees are arranged around the quality of the vendor's performance.

- The root cause of vendor failures is jointly found/remedied.

- The vendor's performance achievements are recognized.

- Continuous improvement is expected, with vendors involved.

nancials, company management depth, acquisition potential and vendor relationship exit strategies (to avoid contractor dependency situations). Sometimes the unit did research on emerging technologies to get a sense of the optimal time to buy into a technology. The result was ever more productive IT investment decisions.

In simple terms, each supplier or contractor is considered part of the IT function's customer experience and, through the IT VRM process, their performance is measured using the same quality metrics as are used by each IT function. The relevant IT function and the supplier/contractor must jointly develop these quality measures. Missed quality targets are seen as joint issues, and the root cause for them is jointly sought. And payment to contractors/suppliers can eventually be based upon their performance against specific quality metrics.

A Better Customer?

So, had I come around to the "hold their feet to the fire" method? No, this was a far more sophisticated approach that stressed relationships over antagonism. For example, the VRM unit wanted to improve on the six weeks that it typically took to place an order for a desktop or laptop PC and install it. Some of the VRM staff met with the vendor and learned that a small volume commitment would allow the vendor to "stack" its product locally for ready shipment—an easy fix that benefited both parties. As a result of this small change, the PC order-to-install time dropped to seven days (including weekends). Instead of holding their feet to the fire, we had just become a better customer.

With an IT VRM unit, we were able to make outside contractors and vendors more of an involved partner in the success of the IT function and its clients. And when the contractors "get it," their performance improves. Recognition occurs. Metrics are raised and an overall continuous performance improvement process actually sets in and becomes expected. And when you get vendors involved to the point that they care about your success as much as you do, another benefit of this approach surfaces: Vendors voluntarily begin making improvements in their offerings to better achieve the jointly required outcome. While this last benefit can be a bit competitive at times, it is irreversible. And it is priceless.

If I were asked about the likelihood of using the "just nuke 'em" approach to attain this level of vendor harmony and partnership, I'd probably respond with some sort of example involving a snowball and a blowtorch. I'd also have to point out that as the above "part of it, proud of it" method is more certain and proven, why would anyone try?

CHAPTER 7

Tell Your Story Plain to Win Over the Business Managers

> *Not so long ago, going into a meeting and hearing a CIO speak in terms that business people could relate to was as startling as it was refreshing.*

The story that follows was not my direct experience, but one told to me by a senior vice president at a company I had once worked at. As such, it's a good illustration of how IT is generally perceived, and how it can position itself as an equal partner in the business's growth:

Sometimes, something you dread can end up being a pleasant surprise. Would you believe me if I told you that, for me, one very memorable occasion like that involved a senior executive committee session at which the new CIO did a presentation called "Yesterday, Today and Tomorrow"?

I had a sinking feeling before heading over to the boardroom. As a high-level general manager reporting to the COO, my attendance at the SEC session was expected, but I had already seen large chunks of my life eaten up by "meant to impress" PowerPoint presentations. I tried to think of a good excuse that would set me free, but none of the ones I thought of sounded plausible, even to me.

As I settled in—in the rear and near the door, just in case—I noted the arrival of the "terrible twosome," a couple of senior executives who were openly referred to as "Crank" and "Grinch." In fact, they liked their nicknames and lived up to them every chance they got. Well, I thought, they will soon make short work of the CIO.

Not that we had any reason to have it in for this particular CIO. In the short time she had been on board, she had made it a point to meet with all of the SEC members, however briefly, asking for suggestions from them on how to make improvements to their IT support, and telling them to let her know personally if something needed her immediate attention. Whenever possible, she looked into business issues pertinent to various SEC members. All of that, we agreed, had been a good first step. But to many on the SEC, all CIOs were insufficiently tuned in to business priorities, were unrealistic about spending and tended to talk in a language foreign to most business people.

Now, having been introduced by the COO, she rose and walked over to the projection screen. But instead of taking the remote control and commencing a PowerPoint presentation, she stood directly in front of the darkened projector and started to address the assembled group.

The CIO Speaks

"I've been here three months now," she said after some preliminaries, "long enough to know where IT is today and to form some ideas about where IT needs to be in the future in order to help support the enterprise. I've got some thoughts about what IT should be doing and where it should be investing, but I need your guidance on these matters. The important thing to me is that IT serve the business, and you on the SEC should be the ones who make the final decisions about that. My job really is to scope out the technological prospects and articulate the benefits for you. After that, I need you to tell me which ones we should focus on."

Okay, so far so good. No one was looking sleepy.

At this point, each of us was given a single page containing only a few topics.

The CIO continued. "My department is the place in the enterprise where IT is planned, built and run," she said, before proceeding to give the IT function a kind of "productivity report card" in each of these performance areas, using business terms like "avoiding cost," "improving service" and "increasing revenue." The grades she assigned to each area seemed objective, honest and fair, and she patiently explained how she had arrived at each of them.

By now, I could see a lot of people in the room nodding in agreement, but I could also see that Crank and Grinch were getting ready to pounce.

And pounce they did. Crank, who was the CFO, took the first shot; "If you expect to make investments to deal with some of the things you feel need attention, where are we supposed to get the funds?" Not waiting for an answer, Grinch, who was the general counsel, piled on with, "Usually, when we make investments or pay a bill, we know what return we will receive. How will you provide that to us?"

The CIO directed our attention to that single page we each held in our hands, which turned out to be a list of proposed actions, subject to the SEC's approval. Each was targeted to deal with a specific IT area needing attention. The CIO proceeded to review each one in turn. Those that had no immediate investment impact she was already undertaking. Others did require investment, and she filled us in on why they were urgent, quantifying the benefits of addressing them immediately. In response to the concerns raised by Crank and Grinch, she told us that the cost to shareholders would be much higher if nothing were done, but then she backed up this claim by explaining her reasoning, evaluating the risks involved and providing some general numbers.

Echoing Grinch's terminology, she said, "Looking at some of these investments as bills to be paid is actually very useful. You know, anytime you fail to pay a bill on time, the amount you owe goes up. These investments are like that. What is different is that there is also increased risk to our business performance because of delays in taking action." And then she added, "As far as the fairly rapid and ever-increasing amount that it will take to settle, this could also be considered detrimental from a shareholder perspective. Again, each of my proposed actions is subject to SEC approval, and I will be glad to add whatever knowledge I can to the information I've presented to you today."

No more questions. Even Crank and Grinch sat back and seemed eager to hear what more she would have to say.

On to Tomorrow

That was when she got to IT's future. It would be based, she said, on a simple theme. The business units that her IT function served would be treated as real clients. Not "captive clients" or even "virtual clients." They would have a choice as to who satisfied their IT needs. She would immediately undertake the benchmarking of each IT service her function provided—against other commercial alternatives. If an IT service could be provided by others cheaper, faster or better by some qualitative measure, she would take the initiative to make the better alternative work for the enterprise. While she would not support the farming out of strategic IT ser-

USE IT'S BENEFITS TO WIN OVER OTHERS

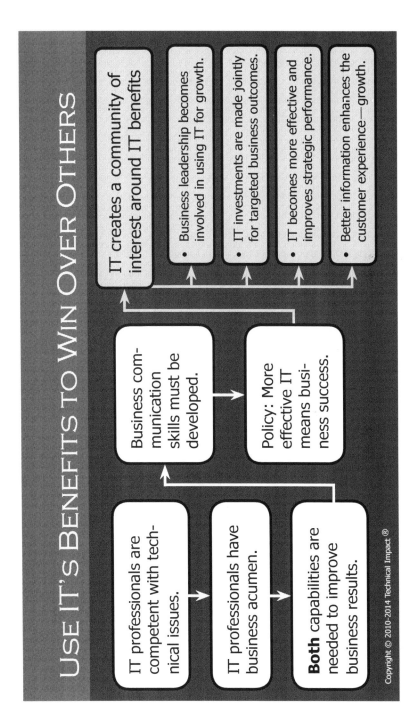

IT professionals are competent with technical issues.

IT professionals have business acumen.

Both capabilities are needed to improve business results.

Business communication skills must be developed.

Policy: More effective IT means business success.

IT creates a community of interest around IT benefits

- Business leadership becomes involved in using IT for growth.
- IT investments are made jointly for targeted business outcomes.
- IT becomes more effective and improves strategic performance.
- Better information enhances the customer experience—growth.

vice areas, she asserted, "If our IT function makes no profit, I believe (and I'm a stockholder too) we should certainly know why we can't deliver our services to your businesses cheaper, faster and better than any alternative."

She also had plans for IT to position itself as a proactive partner to each business unit, so well attuned to each unit's needs that it would from time to time be able to spot ways that technology could be deployed in new ways to help the unit achieve its critical success factors. She foresaw this arrangement as a means for IT to find new ways to avoid cost and improve service, but she thought there was a good chance that some of them might just increase revenue as well. "Removing the fact that IT cannot make a profit, I ask you to please still view us as a targeted business within a business," she said. "One that grows its market share through client-focused performance and innovation. One that has staying power, and one that you could even imagine investing in." And finally, "I believe that if we value our IT service function that way, it will respond to that challenge and take increasing pride in its own strategic contribution to the enterprise. It's my sense that this is an outcome we would all prefer. I'm also convinced that our shareholders will see improved results from this approach as well."

She concluded by saying that she would be grateful for feedback on her proposals, adding that she would like to give similar short presentations every ninety days or so in order to keep the SEC current regarding what IT was doing on behalf of the enterprise's shareholders.

All of this happened in less than thirty minutes. "All killer, no filler," I thought.

All eyes turned to the COO. "There's no reason to postpone action on this," he said. "Yes, no, or let's adjust it— what's your feedback?"

One after another, every SEC member gave the green light, including Crank and Grinch. Those who had further questions were assured by the CIO that she would follow up with each of them later.

The senior vice president who told me this story said he would never forget the eloquence of that presentation, nor the enthusiasm that greeted it. What made it memorable for him, of course, was his long previous experience of listening to IT managers spout jargon, talk about technical things in technical ways, and lose their audience with every word. I've had to endure a few presentations like that myself, and more than once, I've heard senior general managers quote Molière on their way out the door: "That must be wonderful; I have no idea of what it means."

The good news for all those general managers is that the wellspoken CIO who is the hero of this particular story is not alone. IT folks are becoming better business communicators every day. After all, "what it means" is not that complex, if the right language is considerately used.

CHAPTER 8

You Think You Don't Need Buy-in?

> *The reward of arrogance is to know you're right as you go down in flames.*

Travel being what it is, I decided that I had had enough of being an IT consultant, and I accepted a position running a corporation's IT operations function, reporting to the CIO.

But on some level, I hadn't really decided to stop being an IT consultant. I figured I could take what I had done on all of my engagements and apply it to my new job.

I had been a consultant long enough for it to become ho-hum, and for me to become arrogant. The job seemed to promote these developments. We had a template, and we stuck to it, domestic or international. I would go in with the assumption that the IT organization was dysfunctional (why else would an outsider be called in?), and after just half an hour with the general manager who had contracted for the IT review, with no contact at all with the staff, I'd be lining up my recommendations. Nothing ever interceded to tell me

I might be wrong to do this. Time after time, my hunches were borne out by what I found later during the review.

My final reports all said pretty much the same thing: "If you want to accomplish this, then you have to do that. If you don't know how to do that, you have to learn how to do that. If you don't know how to learn that, you can have someone like us teach you." Get on plane. Repeat.

At the new job, at least, the IT operations function seemed to be in pretty good shape. There was a forthright management team, and no one was afraid of work. Dusting off my trusty consultant's microscope, I began the process of looking at the details.

I found some wear and tear here and there in terms of folks who were a little overworked and undertrained for the work that they were assigned. A boost in head count and some training bucks should fix that. Mainframe and network capacity margins? Working, but way too thin. No capacity plan. Some midyear budget relief should fix that. Single points of failure? My, my, we can't have that. A little more budget relief was surely understandable. PC help desk? Swamped. Why? No training in the business units when new desktop software was issued without warning. Because administrative and clerical staff couldn't use the new software properly, business unit productivity dived, big time. Why? If the software deployment was a surprise, the PC help desk couldn't help folks use it. The help desk folks weren't trained, and so trouble tickets mounted. Gee, we'll need some more training funds, plus some additional staff and overtime money to fix this. You get the idea.

Next, I made an urgent appointment with the CIO to discuss my findings and plan of action.

He listened for about five minutes before asking, "So what do you propose?"

I handed him my summary of areas needing attention and what it would take in dollar terms to make them right.

He read it carefully, taking long enough for me to actually consider taking my leave. Then he put down the paper, took off his glasses and looked directly at me. I had a sinking feeling that this was not going to be fun.

"So," he said, "let me get this straight. I've hired a new director of IT operations, right?" I said, "Yes," because that would be me.

"So, now I get to carry your emergency financial needs in to the executive finance committee and get a huge amount of money to fix problems in my IT operational unit that I should have known about in the first place. Am I right?" I said, "I didn't intend for this to reflect . . ."

"Let me tell you something," he interrupted, and I could tell he was just warming up. "Over the last five years, I've had to claw every dime in my modest budget personally out of the hands of executive management and the finance committee. And do you know what?" He didn't wait for a response. "They didn't give a damn about their underinvestment in IT for the previous five years. As a matter of fact, as a percentage of overall profit, my budget is the highest it has ever been. And you want me to somehow go and get you a nice chunk to add to that, midyear, to fix more things that I should have already fixed with my existing budget?"

He went on this way for about twenty minutes. I couldn't help feeling that my hair was on fire and the only way he would let me put it out was with a hammer.

Humbled

When I was finally released from this tongue lashing, I returned to my office to review the situation. The CIO's points were all valid, but the problems that I had uncovered were

IT'S ABOUT THE SHAREHOLDER

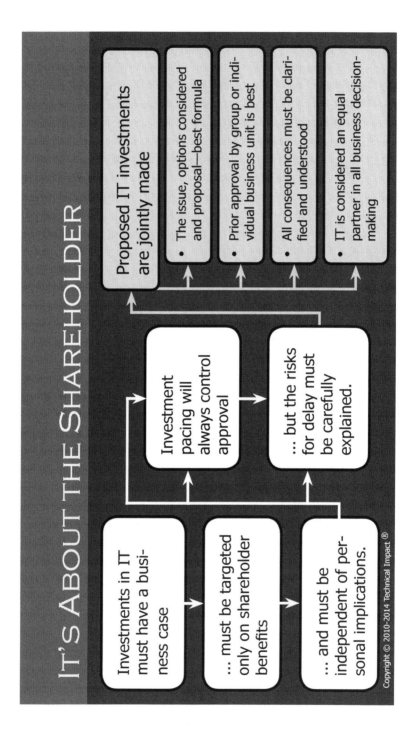

Investments in IT must have a business case

... must be targeted only on shareholder benefits

... and must be independent of personal implications.

Investment pacing will always control approval

... but the risks for delay must be carefully explained.

Proposed IT investments are jointly made

- The issue, options considered and proposal—best formula
- Prior approval by group or individual business unit is best
- All consequences must be clarified and understood
- IT is considered an equal partner in all business decision-making

equally real and in need of attention. Without additional resources, things would worsen. Gradually, I realized that my
error had been my arrogance, and it came to me then that I
needed to help the CIO bring these needs to senior management's attention without any negative reflection on anyone.
There was no need to cast blame; business needs change. IT
support and capacity must reflect what's happening in the
business or unpleasant financial consequences will arise in
due course.

With a little research, I saw that the best way to express
IT's needs and make a plea for the required investment to
deal with them was surely in stockholder terms. Together
with the CIO, I needed to explain in the language of business people how each of these IT investments would help us
avoid cost, improve productivity or service, or increase revenue. From my modest research, I knew that this was called
"the business case."

I had a very different attitude on my second trip to the
CIO's office to talk about the need for IT investment. This
time, we worked out the business case for each area, and
when we met with the financial committee, the CIO gave
me what air cover he could. In my presentation, I noted that
the company could choose not to deal with these problems,
but delay would carry risks. The important thing was that
the company's decision-makers know about them. Throughout, there was never any suggestion that the CIO should
have seen these problems coming and done something about
them. Far more relevant was that he had sought me out and
brought me aboard in order to help the company deal with
such IT productivity issues. By presenting all this information to the committee, I was only acting in accordance with
my assigned function. By presenting the information in the
form of business cases that spelled out the risks in terms of

looming costs or revenue reductions, I was better assuring the best outcome.

Flies and Honey

Since then, I have always been on guard against arrogance in myself. I realized that there was nothing to be gained if in the course of seeking buy-in for something, I implied that the need I was describing was due to the personal failure of someone else or the result of someone's misguided intent. In fact, such a negative approach will always be noticed, and will always reflect poorly on the person using it. Coming at it from another direction, just recall that old bromide about flies and honey. Give a nod to those who got things to where they are and they are likely to step up and help out as you propose new actions for even better results in the future. That is the sort of support you just can't buy.

And to lean on another old bromide, people find an emphasis on opportunities more attractive than a focus on problems. I have found in business that people will jump at opportunities and steer clear of problems. Show them your problems in terms of opportunities, and they will sign on and even share ownership with you. That puts you in a great position, because I've always found that the broader the ownership, the better the outcome.

But I have to confess that despite my best efforts to knock the arrogance out of myself, I sometimes approach things with the wrong attitude. I wish it weren't so, but when it happens, I'm comforted by the fact that I have good company, because I recognize my situation in this quote from Molière: "It infuriates me to be wrong when I know I'm right."

CHAPTER 9

A Tale of Two CIOs

> *In which the business masses rise up and stage a coup against an arrogant IT leader.*

Do you think that what you hear about IT needing to be responsive to the business it serves just doesn't apply to you and your IT department?

Do you feel that business managers who complain about runaway IT spending and opaque IT priorities simply don't get IT?

Do you believe that IT should be the final word on anything related to technology because, quite frankly, technology decisions should be based on technological considerations?

If those are your views, then it is very likely that your career in IT management will be short and unsatisfactory. You are, in fact, very much like a politician who has lost touch with the people and can't see it coming when an election finally turns against him. What you need, I would offer, is the ability to see things from the perspective of the business managers you serve.

To help you out with that, I present the following story, which was told to me by a business unit executive vice president who hoped it might be useful to others.

※

The EVP could feel his temper rising and reflected that this feeling of helpless anger was the one thing the company's IT function seemed able to reliably deliver.

His direct reports all knew that IT was a thorn in his side, but at the business unit staff meeting that had just concluded, each one of them had in turn pressed that thorn a little deeper, and now he was squirming.

The first to pick up the theme was his CFO, who reported that corporate had let it be known that the cost to their business unit to cover the expense of the centralized IT function was expected to increase yet again. The reason? More IT capacity was urgently needed. It had been this way for four years now, ever since that new IT director had been hired and given the inflated title of "chief information officer." IT capacity was always increasing, at great expense, and it was never enough.

The news of still another increase in the tribute paid to IT was enough to set off all the other direct reports, who all complained that the profitability of the business unit was being stolen by the central IT function for vague and incomprehensible reasons.

They asked questions that they had already asked many times before: "How are we expected to stay competitive and still make a profit with IT stealing our margin?" "Why don't we know what we're getting for the ever-growing IT expense we must pay?" "Business publications all say that the IT price-performance ratio is improving, so, why don't our IT costs decrease?" He couldn't ignore them. These were solid professionals that he had groomed over the course of decades. But the CEO was firmly in the CIO's corner, and the EVP had never seen a clear course of action that he could take to improve the situation.

Now, though, it occurred to him that the centralized IT function was taking the focus and momentum out of his business unit. Profits were being sucked away, and his managers were starting to become obsessed with the situation, unable to fully focus on managing the business. He was long practiced in taking the actions that needed to be taken to benefit the shareholders, and he could see clearly now that reining in IT was something that had to be done. How to do that, though?

There was a time when IT funding had been predictable and grew in step with the business. Back then, there had only been a director of management information systems (MIS), who reported to the corporate CFO. But the MIS director had retired, and the CEO and chairman went out and recruited a "star" in the IT industry, who was to have a "C" title and report directly to the CEO. Even then, the EVP had had misgivings. It worried him that the IT function would now have no involvement from business unit management.

Seeing them together at senior executive committee meetings, the EVP thought that the new CIO had the CEO and chairman enthralled. He was a captivating speaker, in his way, though the EVP could never say afterwards just what it was he had talked about. He whizzed through complicated diagrams, using phrases that were unfamiliar to him, but doing it in a way that implied that everyone should already know what they meant. His presentations were peppered with terms like "kernel," "fourth-generation relational operator languages," "gestalt," "pixels per inch," "third normal form," "compressed self-checking packets," "front-end processors" and "channel extenders," along with enough acronyms to make one's head swim.

Occasionally the EVP was able to throw in a straightforward question like, "How can what you are talking about benefit my business unit?" "That's an excellent question," the CIO would respond, and then he would take the question off the table by suggesting that he explain it one-on-one after the session. But a real answer was never forthcoming because the CIO's boss was happy with what he was doing.

The increases in funding had started immediately, with the CIO arguing that his predecessor had not invested in IT properly. "It's just capital," the CEO would say. The EVP stopped waiting to hear any mention of return on investment.

The expenditures had become huge after the CIO had insisted that IT needed to be housed in its own brand-new IT center. Again, the EVP fumed that this project seemed aimed at addressing zero corporate needs; its one purpose, as far as he could tell, was to feed the ego of the CIO.

Now, resolved to take action, the EVP decided that his first step should be to try to understand the IT function better. That new IT center was located in a suburb that he passed on his way home from work, so why not leave early and drop by for a visit?

It was still mid-afternoon when he arrived, but the door was locked. Special passkeys were required to gain entrance. He pressed the bell, and a security guard poked his head out. The EVP identified himself as a member of the senior executive committee and a business unit executive vice president. The guard was unimpressed. His orders were that no one without a passkey could enter unescorted, and such visits had to be arranged in advance through the office of the CIO. The EVP called the CIO's office, but he got voice mail.

This was all in keeping with what he was beginning to see

as the arrogance of IT under the direction of this CIO. Here I am, he thought, the manager of the business unit that had paid for about 65% of the cost of the IT center, and I can't even get my foot in the door to have a look at what I helped pay for.

But he did make the proper arrangements for a tour, and when he showed up on the appointed day, he was escorted around the IT center by a junior IT manager. The IT manager pointed out areas dedicated to network operations, applications development, database management, help desk, mainframe computer, disk arrays, etc. No phones rang anywhere. The term "isolated" popped into the EVP's head, and it stuck there when his questions about how the business units received value from various areas were answered with, "No one ever asked that before." Well, I'm asking, he thought, and it's high time we got some real answers. Heading back to his car, he thought that he had seen some impressive technology but had met not one person who gave even the slightest hint that he knew how the enterprise made money, with or without IT.

At the same time, the EVP had a growing sense that he was not alone in feeling so overwhelmingly frustrated by IT's ascendancy. Yes, in the first months of the CIO's tenure most of the other business unit managers had been very patient and seemed to think that asking him pointed questions was disrespectful. But as the years crawled by and the money kept flowing away toward IT, they had all joined in. Nowadays, they were all tough on the CIO at SEC sessions, peppering him with questions such as "The IT function is getting more and more costly to the enterprise each year. How do we know we are getting value for money?" Business unit managers were being asked to make cuts in market research, call center follow-up, promotional channels and more, but the

Team Conduct Is an IT Leadership Principle

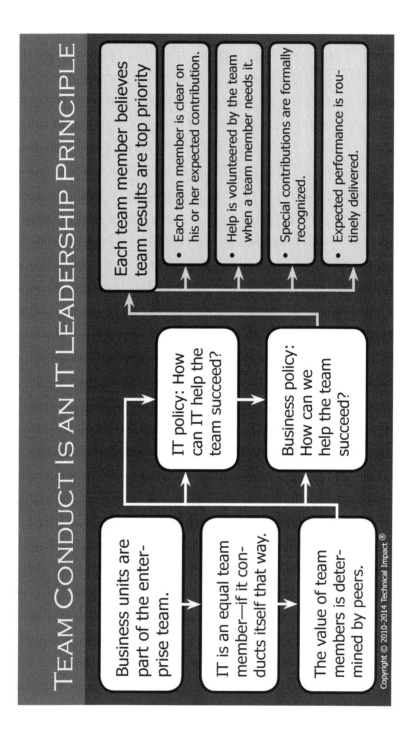

Business units are part of the enterprise team.

IT is an equal team member—if it conducts itself that way.

The value of team members is determined by peers.

IT policy: How can IT help the team succeed?

Business policy: How can we help the team succeed?

Each team member believes team results are top priority

- Each team member is clear on his or her expected contribution.
- Help is volunteered by the team when a team member needs it.
- Special contributions are formally recognized.
- Expected performance is routinely delivered.

IT budget always went in one direction: up. Discontent had reached the point that the CEO felt compelled to request that the CIO pull together a presentation that would settle the question of just what the value of IT was. But the promise of that move quickly evaporated, as the presentation kept getting postponed. It ended up being just a new way for the CIO to stonewall his SEC antagonists, since he could now tell them that he had received a request to deal with that very issue from the CEO and his comprehensive response would be forthcoming. Except that it never arrived. It was around that time that the CIO began to miss some SEC sessions.

Now, the EVP thought that it would be a good idea to touch base with his potential allies. He met with each member of the SEC individually and was shocked to discover that they had actually jumped past him in their feelings of frustration. Some of them had quietly looked into decentralizing their portion of the IT function. One particularly outspoken business unit manager advocated taking bids as if they were going to farm out all of IT. "We don't have to actually farm it out," he said. "But at least then we could compare our costs to some alternatives and get some leverage to deal with our own situation."

With a promise from every business unit manager that they would back him up, the EVP managed to get a special session of the SEC called to address the vitally important issues of IT cost and declining IT performance.

At the special session, it all came raining down, but not on the head of the CIO, who once again hadn't been able to attend. The CEO took the brunt of it, and he finally seemed to wake up to the extent of the damage that had been done. Feeling embarrassed by the part he had played in the debacle, he told the SEC members that he should have been more responsive and involved in the IT situation.

After that session, the CIO and the company quickly parted ways. He immediately assumed a similar position at another company; he must have seen the ax about to come down on his neck. Maybe he hadn't been able to attend the special session because he was already at a job interview.

Shortly after the CIO's departure, the CEO asked the SEC, "What do we look for in a replacement?" That prompted an earnest discussion, resulting in this conclusion: "We need a CIO who is a business-oriented communicator and as concerned about shareholder results as we are."

To assure that happened, a new recruiting process was devised. Business unit managers took part in interviews, and the SEC made the final recommendation.

The new CIO quickly demonstrated that IT was on a new path. He told the SEC that he wanted to get his success criteria from them, and then went through a short process to get agreement on each item comprising the criteria.

He also asked for the SEC's blessing to foster a new IT culture, one in which users would be called clients, IT would focus on business processes rather than technology, IT processes would be measured, IT would be accountable, IT would be proactive, and IT initiatives would target moving the business strategy forward.

Endorsement.

The CIO then set out to benchmark the cost of each IT service. His analysis showed that some IT services compared well to outside providers, but several exceeded what it would cost to purchase the service commercially. The CIO cut costs in those areas, and overall IT performance went into an ongoing continuous improvement cycle. It was the beginning of a long period of prosperity for the company, marked by an IT department that was responsive and growing in tandem with the business.

❧

So, which sort of IT manager are you? If you are the type who tries to build a fiefdom where technology rules and business objectives are never discussed, you might manage, even today, to find employment for a while. But over the years, business managers have become less likely to tolerate that sort of thing. If you are the type who strives to make all of IT's actions be responses to real business needs and who understands the company's goals and how technology can help achieve them, you become an involved partner with the business. And you will have a growing sense of accomplishment and reward in your long and fulfilling career.

And perhaps years later, your colleagues from the business side will be telling tales in which you are their partner in business success instead of an isolated, if impressive, technologist.

CHAPTER 10

Chasing Perfection

> *Perfection only comes when performance continuously improves.*

The CIO had caught me unprepared, and it showed.

"Can you improve what your IT applications software development organization is doing for my IT function and the company?" he asked.

"Is there a problem?"

Wrong response. In fact, not a response at all, as he pointedly noted.

I managed to say that my software development function was always seeking to improve what it does for the IT function and the company.

"Good," he said, "but I want to know what specific improvements have been made in IT software applications development and what more will be achieved, and exactly when each will happen."

Surprised, I told him that I needed some time to get the facts.

He granted the time, but he also made it clear that what he was asking for should never be a surprise to me in the future.

Thus did this new CIO launch me into one of the great lessons of my career. In the next several days, I was to learn things about the essence of leadership. Having spent years in software development, I had become comfortable. But I was no longer a programmer, a systems analyst, a systems programmer, a database administrator, a project manager or a section manager, all roles I had filled in the past. I was director of application software development and maintenance, a leadership position. And leaders, he was telling me, should never feel comfortable. They need to always ask questions and to have answers ready when questions are put to them. They need to know where their group has been and where it's going. And they need to be able to speak about those things in specific, not hazy and generalized, ways.

Not that any of this was clear to me as I walked down the hall mulling over what the CIO had said. I was thinking, in fact, that his request was somewhat confusing. Yes, he was new, but he was already aware that my group had made many improvements over time in terms of formalizing requirements, adopting standards, using new rapid application development techniques and prototyping tools, and adopting rigorous configuration management and regression testing processes. So, what was he really asking for?

I figured I could give him a PowerPoint presentation and be done with it. I would recap the past with some slick slides and finish off with my intentions to adopt newer productivity tools, "time boxing" them by quarter over the coming year or so.

While this kept me occupied for a while, I was at the same time nagged by the thought that after the "coming year or so" was explained, the CIO was likely to say, "Okay, what then?" And I had no answer.

Going around and around, I asked myself what the CIO would like to tell his management about his function now and in the future. As I pondered what I should be saying, terms like "effective," "performance" and "productive" kept popping into my head. They seemed very business-like to me, and I couldn't shake the thought that none of my suggested technical initiatives connected with them.

Then it hit me: I'd gone native. I'd become an inwardly directed software development technology practitioner. I didn't know how to express my initiatives and the pride I had in them in a way that my manager could relate to or communicate to his management. Worst of all, I'd been unable to provide any kind of context for the happenings in my organization that would make future benefits understandable.

I made an appointment with the CIO and told him that I had assembled most of the detail for my report but was struggling to present it in a way that would produce what he needed. "What do you have in mind?" he asked. "I want to talk about my function's past, present and future in terms of cost-effectiveness, improved performance and improved productivity," I told him. "And I would like to add an assessment of how our internal clients view us." He graciously extended my deadline, which gave me the assurance I needed that I was at last on the right track.

Native No More

Now the hard part began. I assembled my direct reports, and we started trying to fill in the blanks. It may have been dumb luck, but our "hip-shot" approach to doing technical things better over time had somehow fit the improvement trend we'd laid out. Not that our progress was dazzling by

VALUE-FOCUSED CONTINUOUS IMPROVEMENT

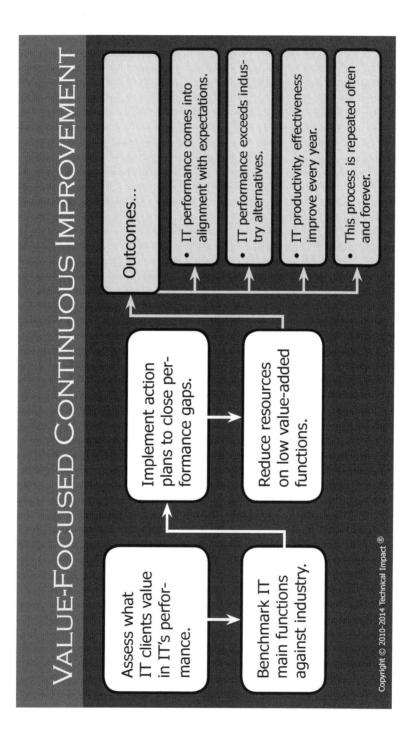

Assess what IT clients value in IT's performance.

Benchmark IT main functions against industry.

Implement action plans to close performance gaps.

Reduce resources on low value-added functions.

Outcomes…

- IT performance comes into alignment with expectations.

- IT performance exceeds industry alternatives.

- IT productivity, effectiveness improve every year.

- This process is repeated often and forever.

any means, but we had made reasonable progress. The past and present portions of the report started to fall into place. The future was the sticking point, and we were pretty thin on what our internal clients thought about us; we only had some informal information and a few e-mailed kudos. That was when inspiration struck one of my direct reports. "You know," he said, "knowing our weaknesses is a strength. The CIO has endorsed the idea of assessing how our internal clients view us, and we currently have very little to go on. So, one of our future improvements should be to more formally assess our clients' perceptions." We all cheered this idea and realized that such assessments would generate actions for the things that needed attention.

From there, we focused on the term "quality," which stimulated still more ideas for the future. Best practices, benchmarking, continuous improvement, reducing cycle time, doing more within each cycle, adjusting what we thought was quality in the past to what our clients now consider quality. We had burst through a dam, and our thoughts were flowing freely. But I was still nagged that we had no desired outcome reference point to build toward. "All right," I could imagine the CIO saying, "fixing weaknesses and closing gaps sound good. But against what goal? Why should the enterprise care?"

Our problem, I could now see, was that "IT quality" and "IT excellence" could be defined in different ways from different perspectives. Not only had we not defined them, but we had not run these definitions by our stakeholders.

We started to talk to the leadership of our internal clients in order to put the question to them directly. With each of them, we summarized what we had accomplished for them in the past, declared our intention to adopt continuous quality improvement initiatives and vowed to develop their applications on time and within budget. But, we added, what more could we do to help them succeed?

The issues tumbled out, and many of them were things we never would have targeted for improvement without these discussions. Although many of the leaders at first didn't believe we were sincerely trying to build a new relationship with them, several ended up being enthusiastic about what a new partnership between us could result in. They started sharing their customer acquisition and retention cycles in the hope that it would improve our appropriate responsiveness, and they eventually asked us to engage in discussions that would help them see how IT could assist them in becoming more productive. We took notes and scheduled a series of follow-up sessions to deal with each suggested improvement area.

We had gone from a vague goal of IT productivity improvement to a realization that, while it was essential, such improvement was meaningless if it was divorced from the larger business issues.

I realized that I had finally broken through to see things more clearly from the CIO's perspective, and that we had what we needed to make our report to him. It could have been a less clumsy presentation, but despite our rambling, we knew that he got where we were coming from when he said, "So, you're saying that for you to be successful in your function, your contribution must actually help your clients' businesses succeed?"

Afterward, my direct reports and I added more lessons about IT quality improvement as we dealt practically with each aspect of IT quality. For example, we found that benchmarking by itself could lead to mediocrity; an IT function might measure well against others and yet fall short of what it could have achieved by independently introducing beneficial change. We even suggested new ways to introduce emerging technology to avoid cost, improve service and yes, even increase revenue.

The great debt I owe that CIO was this lesson that has served me well in all the years since: You cannot possibly place a value on the service you provide if you do not talk about it with the people you are ostensibly performing it for. In other words, clear, two-way communication is key to effective leadership. The CIO himself was constantly demonstrating this, and he never gave a presentation to his senior management committee without first meeting with the leadership of each line of business, to make sure the IT function he led was properly aligned with each of their operational and strategic needs.

CHAPTER 11

The CIO You Don't Want to Be

> *If the IT function waits until a crisis to talk to the business side, it will have a hard time finding common ground that will make it easier to solve the problem. And it will confront a lot more crises.*

Sometimes you meet a person who strikes you as an inspiring role model. Other times, you get a role model of a different sort, an example of how not to be. The CIO I had just spent an hour with was definitely the second type.

A corporal in a general's uniform, I thought to myself. I had found out earlier that he had never actually developed any applications software in his career, and he certainly didn't appear to know how to direct or delegate such a responsibility now. When it came to the IT framework of plan, build and run, he was quite capable of keeping things running, but he was clueless about planning and building. He probably never should have gotten his position in the first place, and it looked as if I was hired to help assure that he didn't stay in it much longer.

This was during my consulting career. I had been engaged by the managing director of a strategic business unit of a large enterprise who was having trouble dealing with the central IT service function. There were many problems, such as IT's failure to meet agreed-upon service levels and not seeming to care. But what had prompted his call to me was the near impossibility of getting software developed or modified. The IT function was unresponsive and bureaucratic, throwing up a stone wall by saying that it would work on applications software development only after the business unit documented the system requirements.

"I don't know what a system requirement is or how to document one," the managing director told me. "And the last time I got my people to try and do that, the IT function returned my write-up months later with a list of things that we'd omitted or that they thought wouldn't work."

His exasperation was rooted in business considerations. "We're losing business," he said. "We know how to address our problems with better technology, yet we're stuck, because this IT bureaucracy is keeping anything from getting done."

After he had filled me in on more details, I had a pretty clear picture of an IT function with a bunker mentality. It's not a rare thing, unfortunately, perhaps because there are so many things that can contribute to it. In some cases, IT simply had a very limited budget and no way to prioritize development expenses, so they raised hurdles to bar against new ones. Other times, IT had been badly burned after diving into a big development project with inadequate specifications. Or it had insufficient resources, or had lost the talent necessary to develop new applications, or was unable to communicate with business units or become involved in business unit issues. No matter the root cause of a bunker mentality, the result was invariably a relationship that verged on adversarial with IT's clients.

The managing director was ready, if necessary, to do an end

run around the in-house IT function to get what he needed. He was confident the CEO would back him up. "Time is our competitors' best friend now, and the CEO knows it," he told me.

I spent some time familiarizing myself with the managing director's system development needs, and then I met with the CIO. What I found was a politically astute, melodramatic and theatrical bully. He was darkly threatening and intent as he asked me about my qualifications, the results I had achieved and the person who had engaged my services. He became less dark when he learned that the CEO knew about my mission.

Apparently believing that he could make all this go away with some carefully phrased happy talk, he told me that his IT function and the business units it served were a team. But his body language suggested that he wanted nothing more than for this meeting to end. My guess was that he was itching to "back channel" the CEO to assess what damage had been done to his career.

I was more amused than irritated by his behavior, mostly because it was so transparent, even though he seemed certain that it was a convincing performance. I didn't let on, though, as I said to him, "I understand that you have a strict policy that internal clients must write up their own system requirements, with no cooperation from IT. I would expect such an approach to delay results. Why do you do things that way?" For me, this was a natural question, because I really couldn't understand how this policy could be deemed a good idea. In my experience, systems requirements are best developed jointly, with IT professionals and business specialists working together. Software can then be delivered in stages depending on priority, so as to avoid high-risk, all-or-nothing, complex implementations.

INTEREST + INVOLVEMENT + INITIATIVE = ALLY

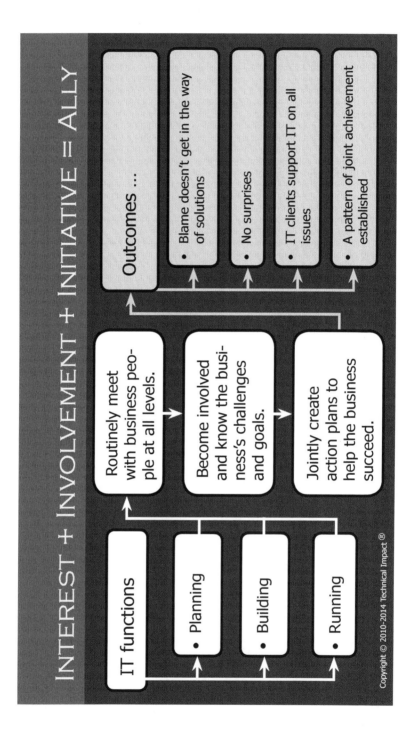

IT functions
- Planning
- Building
- Running

Routinely meet with business people at all levels.

Become involved and know the business's challenges and goals.

Jointly create action plans to help the business succeed.

Outcomes ...
- Blame doesn't get in the way of solutions
- No surprises
- IT clients support IT on all issues
- A pattern of joint achievement established

What this question prompted was amazing to see. First, the CIO questioned every assumption behind my query. Then he wanted me to name my informants and to tell him exactly what they said. Finally, he was keen to know whether he had been mentioned specifically.

I answered him with equanimity (whereas he had answered me not at all), and he then sputtered, "This is a serious issue for me and now that I'm aware of it, I will make it my top priority." To show how serious he took the matter, he added, "When I get to the bottom of this, I may have to start over with new people!"

In short, everything had been a failure on the part of someone other than him, and he would be sure to punish the wrongdoers.

And so, I thought upon taking my leave, this little corporal is going to make sure that heads roll, to demonstrate to all that he is fully in control. It was the completely wrong response.

Options

I had an exit interview with the managing director and two other senior executives from other business units.

"The CIO called and asked me why I hadn't informed him directly about my problems with his team," the managing director told us, more than a little amused. "He said that if he'd known about our delays, he could have avoided all this. I told him that I'd left three messages with his secretary during the requirements-writing debacle without a return call and that I'd noticed that he had signed off on every bureaucratic and time-wasting document in that ridiculous exchange. So, I asked him, how could you not know about this situation? I also told him that he was supposed to be running a client-focused internal corporate service and that the business units were his customers. I suggested that he and his team start treating us that way."

The other senior executives were heartened by the report of this exchange, but it was time to get down to business. The managing director turned to me and asked, "What needs to be done here?"

"I see three options," I said. "First, the CEO could direct the CIO to provide a commercial-grade IT function that plans, builds and runs all IT services at less cost than external contractors. The second option would be to create an exception that would allow business units to make use of external developers when the internal corporate IT function can't provide its service in a timely manner. Finally, there's the option of leaving corporate computer operations—the 'run' piece of IT—centralized while moving all applications software development staff into the business units."

I would have added that I thought the first option was clearly best, for many reasons, not the least of which was the shareholders' viewpoint. But before I could do so, it became clear that the business managers had already agreed upon a similar course of action.

In the end, the CIO ended up reporting to a new CIO who was proficient in collaboration with the business units the IT function served.

So What?

If you are a CIO who doesn't routinely meet with the heads of every strategic business unit you serve in order to get to know them personally and assess your IT function's performance before there is a crisis, *you are in a career-limiting position.*

You need to remain aware of even the smallest ways you might improve the IT function's contribution to the strategic intent of the enterprise and each business unit within it. You need to stay in contact so that you can be effective in dealing with issues *before they become critical.*

And an overbearing management style is counterproductive and ultimately short-lived, for the simple reason that no one wants to spend time with someone who employs it; they are unpleasant people, incapable of constructively exchanging knowledge and wisdom or building joint focus and momentum. I'm fond of Joel Barker's definition of a leader: "Someone you chose to follow to a place that you would not otherwise go." Even if you have the chops that this doomed CIO was sorely lacking, you should never rely on an overbearing management style. Those who report to managers who employ such an approach never consider them leaders.

CHAPTER 12

Of Operators and Performers

> *There's no getting away from politics in the work-place, but you can survive it.*

There's politics in IT. Are you shocked to hear it? I didn't think so. But it can be negotiated. It comes down to knowing what sorts of people are around you. I'll get to that in a bit, along with some advice for dealing with the bad players, but first let me tell you about two times in my career when politics came to the fore.

Incident Number One

I had just renegotiated a multiyear contract with a major outside IT service provider that would save the company $6 million in each of the next three years. I was feeling confident about my competence as CIO, but at the same time, I saw indications that my days at this company might be numbered. The CEO who had hired me was now leading a rival company. We had been close, and a couple of my peers on the senior management committee had asked me whether

I would follow him. There had even been subtle suggestions that I might be feeding our former CEO information about how our IT function was used to outcompete the competition. It was a baseless suspicion, but it's not easy to remove such a stain even when you're completely innocent. Shortly after my success with the renegotiation, the new president and CEO called me to his office. Once I was there, he cordially congratulated me on my negotiating success. In fact, he said, my performance had been consistently superior, but due to reasons he could not discuss with me, he would have to let me go. My competence was not called into question, and that was gratifying, but I was out of a job anyway.

Incident Number Two

Seeing the executive who hired you move on isn't unusual, of course. When it happened to me another time, I was left reporting to a committee of three senior executives who didn't know what they wanted the IT function to do. They would ask me what I considered to be the best path to take, but my carefully weighed responses would be interrupted by them as they argued with each other. I was being given three competing lists of priorities, and pointing out their contradictions only prolonged the meetings. None of them would give an inch. If they all hadn't had other meetings to attend, those sessions might have never ended. No one can serve two masters, and I found myself with three. I wasn't learning anything, which has always been of great importance to me, and I had the feeling that my situation was going to end poorly, so I began looking for another position. As soon as I found one, I resigned. Again, my performance was not the issue, and even though I had moved on through my own initiative, another change in my career happened because of events I had no control over.

❧

Throughout this book, I champion focusing on performance and developing relationships. But as those two incidents illustrate, even when you do that, you can be hit by the unexpected. But you know what? That's okay. The point is that the proactive competence that I have been preaching will indeed serve you well in the course of your career, even if it can't save you from every bumpy political situation. The truth is that when you run into the sort of trouble that I just described from my own career, you are running up against people who aren't the sort of proactive leader that I advocate. And chances are that when things reach a point where you can't continue to serve a company, it's really for the best that you get on to the next chapter in your career.

Not that you can run away from every job that presents you with uncomfortable politics. You would constantly be on the run. It's actually possible to overcome many political situations. The first step is to learn how to read people.

Two Kinds of People

When it comes to workplace politics, it's helpful to learn how to differentiate the performers from the operators.

Performers are the people whom you to want report to, whom you want to hire for your team and whom you're happy to see among your peers. They have a high standard of behavior, a committed work ethic and a well-developed sense of integrity. You can't identify them by their education; they could be Harvard graduates or high-school dropouts. But they exude knowledgeability about their profession, as well as intelligence. They exist at all ranks, and whether they are in the corner office or a cubicle, their conduct is basically the same. They perform in a consistently superior fashion, giving the impression that they would rather do a good job and have it appreciated than almost anything else. They believe that their efforts will be recognized and rewarded (naïvely so, if they're working for an operator). They might make mistakes, but they are quick to own up to them and waste no time in dealing with them. They learn from their mistakes and never make the same one twice. Performers are also genteel, considerate and effective communicators. They work well with and support others. You can be certain that they will do the right thing even when you are not there to know that they've done it. They are happy to share credit for successes. They honor your belief and trust in them. I admit that all of this sounds too good to be true, but I can give you names.

Operators focus on pleasing upper management, being in control of all aspects of their organization and using any achievement to their utmost advantage. They tend to hire people less capable than themselves, sycophants who can be controlled, mostly by intimidation. That helps assure that upper management won't see anyone more capable to promote or replace them with; by default, they look like the only go-to person in the department. Any direct report who is capable and unintimidated is seen as a threat. If the employees who are perceived as threatening can't be bullied, they are subjected to a campaign of informal new requirements meant to encourage their departure. An operator's ethics can be summed up as "whatever it takes," which means that any good ideas will be appropriated, i.e., stolen. They have no compunction about spending time and resources trying to find out whom to blame for a mistake. Again, educational background is not an indicator, but operators are not knowledgeable about what they do; in their minds, taking training would be an admission that they don't know something. Their management style is reactive, and so they often have to accommodate surprises that would not have happened if they had a knowledgeable strategy in place. Worse, they actually like things this way; they figure that if they are seen to be the first person to throw water on a fire, they will be perceived as a hero, even if they started the fire in the first place. If someone you have pegged as an operator makes you feel important, you can be certain that they need something from you and that the situation is temporary. Operators love to flaunt any symbols of power they accumulate. Even the remote possibility of the limelight attracts them. If they work hard, you can bet that the sole reason is to be perceived by upper management as a performer. They are masters of creative half-truths, innuendo and stalling tactics such as "I'll certainly get back to you on that." At bottom, they are very insecure, always scared of being found out. I have seen more than my share, and once again, I have names.

Operating with Operators

I think I'm safe in assuming that most of the people who will read this book are performers; learning from someone else's experiences is not an operator mode of operation. There's no need to tell you anything about how to work with other performers, other than to pay attention and be prepared to learn. But performers need to protect themselves from operators at all levels, whether you report to them or have some on your own team. (It happens to the best of us.)

When it comes to your team, it's essential that you identify the operators and then either change their behavior or replace them. Doing nothing will sap the motivation and momentum of your performers, who may even begin to leave.

Identifying operators who work for you isn't as hard as you might think. I routinely had meetings with all levels of my staff and told the intervening levels of management that

I wanted to deal with the team members directly without their involvement. Any manager who nonetheless showed up at such a meeting was behaving like an operator: Such managers felt compelled to find out who was saying what to me, and they couldn't bear the thought that their reports might be talking about them or how they were treated. If no managers show up but no one at the meeting can suggest any improvements and no one engages in unguarded dialog, you probably have found another operator. Staffers who report to an operator often feel too intimidated to talk honestly even when the operator isn't around. Another good tip-off that someone is an operator is an inordinate amount of self-serving credit-taking. Keep in mind that operators who report to you consider you to be upper management, and operators are always trying to present themselves to upper management as the one worthy and reliable person at their level. Everyone should be allowed to take a bow now and then, but with operators, this tendency is excessive.

If you report to an operator, you have more work of another kind to do, but if you are diligent, you will be left alone and have plenty of time to make good and lasting things happen with your team.

You should start to guard your flank as soon as you suspect that the person you report to is an operator. (You don't have to confirm your suspicion; the precautions that I recommend taking are in themselves innocuous, and if it later turns out that your boss is a performer, no harm done.)

Operators thrive on informality, which makes it easier for them to rewrite history or feign convenient amnesia as they contradict your version of events and agreements. To protect yourself, you must become a master of formality. You have to adopt the rigorous habit, as soon as possible after every meeting, of drafting a concise e-mail that reviews the course of action that was decided on, the direction that was given to you, the exact parameters of any assignment given to you, and time frames that were agreed to. My memos tended to start off with a statement such as "I have already begun to implement the actions we discussed at today's meetings, but before my people get too far along, I want to ensure that I haven't misunderstood anything." Then I would go on to outline everything as I recalled it, and I would *always* close with words such as "Please let me know if anything in this e-mail does not reflect what you understood."

Sometimes, you'll have to take action before you even leave the meeting. Your boss might give you a new assignment that you realize your team doesn't have the resources to handle because of earlier projects that already have you at maximum capacity. (If your boss really is an operator, then he or she probably already knows this and is simply seeing what can be gotten away with.) When it happens, you have to speak up, no matter what heat you might get for doing so. Tell your boss that you can probably handle this new assignment, though it could mean rearranging things and finishing some current projects later than planned. Be reassuring—"If we can handle it, consider it done." Then do the e-mail thing again in a day or so to inform your boss that unless you can agree on a way to restructure existing priorities, the new assignment will have to wait. Again, end with words to the effect of "Please let me know if anything about this is not clear."

If your boss is an operator, he or she will push back on all this documentation and suggest that all of the follow-up isn't necessary. That is pretty much confirmation of operator status. Which means, of course, that you should *not* go along with the suggestion. Your e-mails are an insurance policy, making it much more difficult for an operator to pull you

GET WHAT YOU AND YOUR TEAM DESERVE

Performers are the people you trust and want to work with.

Operators are the ones that you must protect yourself from.

Performers prefer formality and documented facts.

Operators thrive on informality, which lets them interpret things to suit their purposes.

Being a master of formality will protect you and your team.

- Rigorously document all agreements, time frames and commitments immediately.

- Report on progress at least monthly with independent verification.

- Summarize accomplishments against commitments early on and submit them promptly.

- Your team's rewards will be undeniable.

this way and that, according to whim.

Those initial follow-up e-mails aren't the end of it. As projects move along, you should have your team, on a monthly basis, keep track of the progress of all formally agreed-upon goals assigned them. Six weeks before your annual review (or your probationary period if you're in a new position), summarize everything carefully. Quantify as much as you can. Demonstrate progress against all your goals, showing how you achieved those that were reached and noting when your performance exceeded the target. Don't just say that projects were completed on time, for the agreed cost and as specified; provide the evidence. If your team was called on to handle ever more units of work, spell out their increased productivity. If they received kudos from your clients, forward them. (And it's a good idea to solicit as much praise from your clients as possible.) Then summarize all of this from the shareholder point of view, explaining how your team avoided cost, improved service or increased revenue.

About a month before your review session, send this report to your manager. Explain in a cover note that you thought this outline of the past few months' progress would be a handy guide during the review process. Of course, the operator manager is going to helpfully suggest that you spend your time on projects other than writing up things that the manager already knows all about. Don't be dissuaded. Just say that it was no trouble, because all of this material was generated by your direct reports anyway, as a way to allow you to objectively measure their performance; it was no trouble to gather it all together and send along to your own manager.

Formality is your antidote to operators' behavior, and dispassionately dealing with every exchange with them will serve you well. Even melodramatic, undisciplined bullies know when the evidence is against them.

Yes, these formalities will take some of your time. You'll find, though, that this will be a very small price to pay for making obstacles to your team's achievement simply vanish.

And your team members' recognition and rewards will be undeniable.

CHAPTER 13

Can We Please Get Everyone to Speak the Same Language?

> **Business units have the special capabilities, not headquarters.**

The CEO spoke five European languages fluently, but his chief concern in meeting with me, his new CIO, was that the IT services of this $20 billion telecommunications behemoth, with its major business units in France, Italy, Belgium, Spain and Germany and many others in 24 other countries, were a Tower of Babel.

We were in his Paris office for my initial session with him. He started by reviewing the situation. The enterprise had grown rapidly in recent years, mainly through major acquisitions in several European countries.

But, he said, "when it comes to IT, they just don't get along." Language wasn't really the problem, since he had established English as the official language of enterprise IT, but there were clearly other barriers to cooperation among the various IT units. And cooperation was key to the CEO's plans for making this conglomeration work. He had recently visited each business unit to deliver a clear message: When it comes to IT, we as an enterprise would have to work together and share our knowledge. It made no sense to keep knowledge isolated, so that IT in one part of the enterprise had to learn what IT in another part of the enterprise had already figured out. Such redundancy in IT increases our costs and time to market, and we lose our competitive edge as a result.

Since those visits, though, he had only seen a token gesture here and there. In the main, IT continued to be managed in the same isolated and contained fashion as always, and most of the 4,200 IT professionals in the enterprise talked only to the colleagues they already knew, usually within the same business unit.

What followed this summary of the situation was a beautiful example of leadership. First, the CEO took the blame. "It's partly my doing," he said. "I haven't provided any kind of framework for such an open exchange on IT matters." This was followed by a questioning look that invited me to jump in and save the day. "You certainly know where I'm going with this, don't you?" his look seemed to say. I took the bait and told him that I would visit each major business unit and then present such a framework for his review and approval.

He smiled then, and gave me six weeks.

On the Ground

On each stop of my whirlwind tour of the major business units, I found IT units that were crisp, professional, cooperative and mostly up to date. I was in data-gathering mode, so I tried not to think too much about the framework that would be the actual deliverable. Instead, I concentrated on what I was seeing in each unit. I learned what I could about the individual IT professionals I met and their IT units' proficiencies. From time to time, I was asked polite but direct questions, which allowed me to discuss the challenge we all faced. One of the messages I delivered was that business unit IT staff would eventually participate in forums to help deal with the enterprise issues more collectively. And at each unit, I always managed to ask for ideas. Everyone gave me a vague sense of a willingness to cooperate for the greater good.

The managing directors of the subsidiaries were another matter. They were so uniform in their approach and attitudes that I had to assume that they had talked to each other ahead of my arrival. The irony was that they seemed capable of communicating with each other only for the purpose of ensuring that they wouldn't have to communicate with each other.

They all requested what they called a "small meeting," where they asked for my observations on their unit. I was very positive in my responses, mentioning only a small IT aspect here or there that might need some attention. Then, the real reason for the meeting emerged. To a man, they quietly but emphatically let me know that their business had achieved its leadership position in its market by being totally in control of its own resources. The unstated but unmistakable message was that they were not about to lose any of this control, over IT or anything else, without proof positive that their business situation would somehow improve. All I could think to say was that their position was understandable and that "changes should only be introduced if they are beneficial to the shareholder." Each managing director managed to make sure that as I headed to the airport after these little meetings, it would be clear in my mind that I was the outsider from headquarters.

Piecing It Together

Back in Paris, I read everything I could get my hands on that addressed eliminating enterprise IT redundancy, im-

IT PROGRESS WITHOUT DUPLICATE INVESTMENT

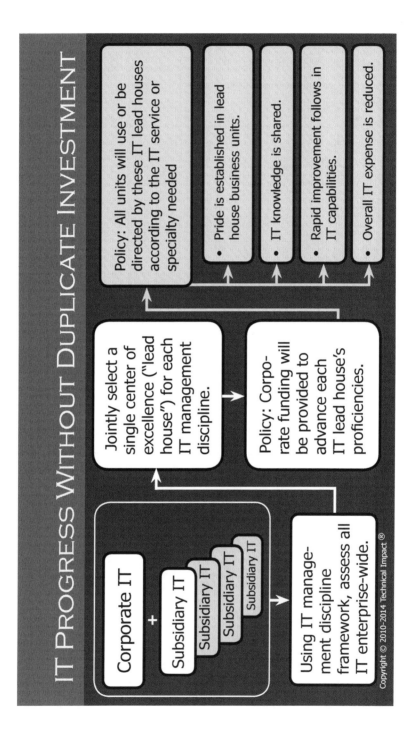

Corporate IT

+

Subsidiary IT
Subsidiary IT
Subsidiary IT
Subsidiary IT
Subsidiary IT

Using IT management discipline framework, assess all IT enterprise-wide.

Jointly select a single center of excellence ("lead house") for each IT management discipline.

Policy: Corporate funding will be provided to advance each IT lead house's proficiencies.

Policy: All units will use or be directed by these IT lead houses according to the IT service or specialty needed

- Pride is established in lead house business units.
- IT knowledge is shared.
- Rapid improvement follows in IT capabilities.
- Overall IT expense is reduced.

proving integration and getting incentives in place to ensure that the process continued across the various vertical market businesses. Taken all together, these materials just didn't deal with the issue in its entirety. I felt that the framework we needed was just outside of my grasp, but I couldn't quite reconcile the demands of the CEO and the managing directors.

I kept working over the problem in my mind, with no real progress to show for it. Then, one day the phone rang. It was two CIOs I had met on my visits, Johann in Antwerp and Albert in Stuttgart. Both of them had let me know that they understood my mission, since they each faced similar rationalization challenges. And in knowing each other and communicating regularly, they broke the enterprise mold.

"It's awfully quiet up there," they said. "We're probably going to be asked pretty soon what you are going to do. So, what shall we say?"

Ah, now here was a dose of reality.

Well, I answered, I feel as if I'm on the verge of figuring it all out, but I just can't make the final connection. Okay, they said, but you shouldn't try to be a solo magician with something this important. "You know, our staffs heard you ask them for their input and their guidance, but they aren't sure that you really want it."

"Then you should definitely spread the word that all suggestions are welcome," I said.

Over the next few days, Johann and Albert helped me rearrange my notes by business unit, and I fired off a memo to each unit. I acknowledged the professionalism I had seen in each unit, and I discussed eleven areas of proficiency, including the level I'd seen in each unit. In some cases, I could say that the unit's proficiency was as advanced as I had seen anywhere. In others, I had to point out shortcomings. I asked for feedback to let me know whether I had been accurate in my assessments, and again I solicited guidance on how best to deal with the rationalization challenge as well as the managing directors' requirement of no loss of control.

And once again, the serendipity of free communication was what moved things forward. My memos found their way to other subsidiaries, which is how Gunnar and Skip, IT professionals from business units in Denmark and France, respectively, came to ask me for a meeting. They felt that they had done nothing less than solve the dilemma by devising an organizational model that would locate centers of proficiency in the business units.

I gave them my full attention.

In simple terms, they proposed that areas of IT proficiency in the enterprise would be identified and jointly reviewed by all IT staff. This review would allow us to select a business unit as the "lead house" for each area of proficiency, depending on the level of IT expertise observed in the business units. Gunnar and Skip foresaw that there wouldn't always be agreement on which unit was worthy of lead house status, but this would cause the contestants to be persuasive. It helped, of course, that there would be plenty of lead house assignments to go around.

The advantage, they explained, was that all business units in the enterprise would look to just one lead house in a particular area of expertise. The lead house could either provide the service to the other business units or tell them how others should provide it. Importantly, if investments were required to improve an area of expertise of a lead house for the benefit of the entire enterprise beyond what would be normally funded by the business unit, then the additional funding would come from corporate.

I realized that Gunnar and Skip had indeed hit on the solution. Their plan was a way to recognize specific IT expertise within business units, avoid redundant IT funding and move IT capabilities into the future, enterprise-wide.

The CEO wanted immediately to bring the idea to the general management team, which consisted of the managing directors. Not one of them breathed a word about loss of control, and with no one able to articulate any downside at all, approval was unanimous. Shortly after that, the plan was rolled out, and I was pleased to see Johann's Belgian unit become the help desk lead house and Albert's German unit the network control center operations lead house. Support was universal, and the momentum became unstoppable when, weeks later, the first projects to bring lead house capabilities to where they should be were promptly funded by corporate.

As a footnote, the overall network of services between all subsidiaries eventually achieved commercial-grade status, and it became another subsidiary business in its own right. In doing so, select resources were extracted from business units, mainly under the direction of Gunnar and Skip. The business units didn't complain about this. They had been part of the whole thing from the beginning.

CHAPTER 14

Getting the Best out of IT Best Practices

> *Wouldn't your company's general management like to see their IT investments working toward better strategic business performance?*

He was the managing director for a strategic business unit that was part of an international enterprise. I first met him when he was looking for an IT project manager.

I found out, though, that the IT system development project he wanted me to manage had been under way for three years and that it was one year late. Worse, it had been reported to be ninety-nine percent complete each month for the past seven months. The individually contracted junior programmers responsible for the software were nowhere to be found. Instead of the industry standard of three seconds or less per transaction, the response time for the system's online functions averaged about four minutes.

I declined the job offer in a letter in which I suggested that systems being built to improve the productivity of his business unit needed their basic requirements established up-front. I went so far as to say that all such IT systems needed to be developed using something called a "systems development methodology," or SDM. I also sent him a couple of books that explained that SDMs were IT best practices.

Three years went by, and suddenly he wanted to see me again. I found him in a new office, occupying a corner of the corporate building fifty floors above Manhattan. He was now the COO of the entire enterprise, reporting to the CEO and chairman.

He started off by filling me in on what had happened after I had said thanks but no thanks. "We did what you suggested in your letter. It cost us a lot to do it, but the darned thing has been running just fine since we redeveloped it using that 'best practices' thing."

He went on, "My responsibilities have changed, and guess what. IT development projects like the one you know about are everywhere I look." He showed me a list of them.

That was why he had called me in. "Here's the deal," he said, getting to his point. "I've created a new IT management position. No one knows exactly what it means yet, but I've clearly indicated enterprise-wide that I'll no longer fund unproductive business unit IT projects unless my new senior director of systems assurance approves them."

Now, I'm somebody who really likes to build things, and here was an opportunity with an interesting twist: to have some influence over building things properly. I had a few concerns about the staying power of such influence, however.

"I know," he said. "You'll be needing these." He handed me an envelope full of his business cards. "I need the word to get out that I will be happy to personally engage anyone that wants to build a system that doesn't do what is needed, is late or is over budget."

With that kind of air cover from the COO, things began to happen. Still, it took about a year for the best practice systems development approach to be fully adopted. IT folks both at corporate and in the business units were required to attend training in how to apply a standard SDM approach to IT development.

While some parts of some IT development projects had to be completely redone, none of them was declared a failure and scrapped. The whole idea was to build on what was already in place whenever possible. The process of "cross-walking" an existing IT development project to the standard SDM approach continued to improve and, at some level, it always worked. IT projects were now usually completed on time, as specified and at the agreed cost. An IT fairy tale, with everyone living happily ever after? Not really. Something was still missing.

Even though we were doing everything right, we still wound up with at least partial "white elephant" systems. They either were awkward to use or had features that were no longer needed by the business that funded them—or both.

The results weren't disastrous. Changes could usually be made to those white elephant systems to make them more usable. But clearly this was not the best use of one's IT investment dollar, either.

Why did this happen? Well, I was too busy cross-walking things to see what was right there before my eyes from the beginning. It was too obvious. We were using system requirements that had been established up to two years before a system was implemented. Despite the passage of so much time, we had done nothing to account for changes in the business that occurred in the meantime.

But aren't SDM approaches built to accommodate changes throughout the development process? Yes, certainly. But under normal conditions and by itself, no SDM, no matter how rigorously followed, can automatically accommodate

Say What You Do. Do What You Say. Prove It. Improve It.

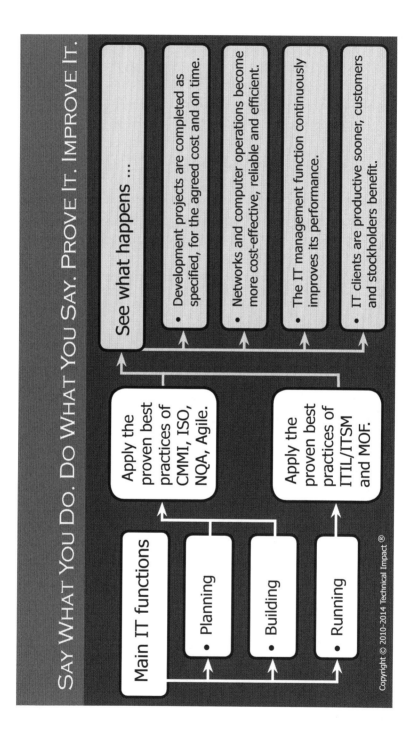

Main IT functions

- Planning
- Building
- Running

Apply the proven best practices of CMMI, ISO, NQA, Agile.

Apply the proven best practices of ITIL/ITSM and MOF.

See what happens …

- Development projects are completed as specified, for the agreed cost and on time.
- Networks and computer operations become more cost-effective, reliable and efficient.
- The IT management function continuously improves its performance.
- IT clients are productive sooner, customers and stockholders benefit.

the sudden acquisition of a new subsidiary with a different business model into the capabilities of a system under development. Ditto the divestiture of an existing company, a suddenly imposed major regulation or a fundamental shift in a business's targeted client segment, client acquisition or retention cycle.

Ultimately, the answer was to adopt a higher-order IT best practice. Individual IT development projects would no longer be thought of as stand-alone "IT transactions." Under a new framework, each IT development effort would be considered an integral and connected part of improving the enterprise's strategic performance through IT. That is, every project would be conceived as a way to avoid cost, improve service and increase revenue at every level. Proposed changes to business or enterprise strategies would now involve something called an "IT impact assessment," which considers not only existing IT operational issues, but IT system development effort issues under way at the time as well. The result? No more white elephants.

Of course, these days (when anything can be Googled), if you were to ask me about IT best practices and where they'd be most usefully applied, I'd start by suggesting something called Capability Maturity Model Integration (CMMI) as a proven framework for predictable system development outcomes and a way to continuously improve IT development productivity (using only Agile project management models). As for IT operational issues, there is the Information Technology Infrastructure Library /Information Technology Service Management (ITIL/ITSM) and the Microsoft Operations Framework (MOF). ITIL/ITSM and MOF are useful frameworks for those in IT operational roles to consider their contributions as part of what their clients experience, with ever more emphasis on process results instead of precise organizational assignments. And these can be built upon, if desired, with the ISO 9000 framework for quality management systems from the international standards organization known as ISO. I've even seen new methods emerge in the last few years that combine all of those approaches into the Malcolm Baldrige National Quality Award structure. ("Say what you do, do what you say, prove it, and improve it.")

Wonderful.

Something you may find useful to keep in mind is the fact that every IT best practice embodies the basic principle to continuously improve strategic business performance through the effective use of IT. The upshot of this should be no surprise to you: Stockholders always consider investing in and managing IT around this principle to be smart leadership.

So what?

Well, if you're in IT management and you haven't yet looked into IT best practices, you may wish to consider how one or more of them might apply to your situation. All IT best practices contain wonderful guidance to show and communicate their value in business terms. Once you're past the awareness and trial steps, you'll wonder, as I did, "Why didn't I do this sooner?"

There's no such thing as job security in IT, of course, but you might consider whether your company's general management wouldn't like to see their IT investments working toward better strategic business performance.

Oh, if you happen to be in general management and you're wondering how to make strategic business sense out of what your folks in IT are doing, perhaps it's time for you to introduce a joint "IT best practices initiative" directed at achieving that very outcome.

Your stockholders are expecting you to do that anyway.

EMPOWERMENT

CHAPTER 15

Leading by Letting Go

> *Improving a dysfunctional IT organization required an embrace of creativity.*

In the course of my career, I've seen my share of dysfunctional IT organizations. One of my most difficult assignments was as CIO for a large county government. It was also one of the best lessons in what it takes to energize IT professionals and serve clients ever more responsively.

As CIO, I found myself the head of a centralized IT function that was rapidly decentralizing. County agencies were creating their own IT support functions, causing some centralized IT functions and resources to go unused. Agencies that were still being supported by the central IT operation found their costs rising, and the duplication of IT resources meant taxpayer dollars were being used inefficiently.

Suboptimal? You bet.

Needing to improve things, I set out to gather the facts. I soon found out that I had a lot to learn.

First, I met with clients who had so far stuck with centralized IT and those who had defected. What, I asked each one, can we do to keep your business or win it back? It wasn't a question any of them was in a mood to answer.

Instead, in meeting after meeting, the clients unloaded on me. They told me how for the better part of the previous ten years they had been unable to routinely communicate with anyone in the centralized IT function. In fact, they had never met with the management team to address IT support strategies or any aspect of the planning, building or running of IT. All I could do was shut up and listen. My attentiveness at least elicited a few comments such as "Okay, you're new. Let's see what you can do for us."

And this turned out to be the fun part of my fact-finding initiative. At least these people were telling me things I needed to hear.

In my many meetings with my IT professional support staff, I came up against complete silence when I asked questions like "What do you need to be more effective and productive?" and "What would you do if you could do anything to improve our services or avoid cost?"

Doing everything I could to eke out a response, I was told things like "We don't need anything" and "We can't decide for management." There was no energy or enthusiasm. Was it fear? Was it me? Was it my predecessor?

My direct reports filled me in. For six years, they said, the management style of the entire IT function could be summed up in the word "control." Nothing was to be communicated to anyone outside the IT function unless the CIO personally approved it. All initiatives needed the CIO's approval, and anyone who championed an initiative that did not reflect positively on the IT function was punished.

Naturally, most IT staffers had decided that the risk of taking any initiative was too high. Those who had tried and had their head handed to them were certainly not going to repeat the experience.

My direct reports and I finally summed up the situation in ten words: "Our clients are leaving us, and our employees don't care." Suboptimal indeed.

But we all believed we could fix both halves of that sentence.

We decided that we had to run the central IT function as a business. Our first step in the "commercialization" of IT was to form a business systems group, with members carefully chosen from each IT function for their excellent communication and interpersonal skills. These skills were then enhanced with even more business communication training.

Given the history of mistrust, it's no surprise that things got off to a slow start. But the BSG team members began to test the waters by making suggestions. Why not benchmark the cost of our services against the alternatives? Shouldn't our clients have an IT services directory showing all that we offer and whom to call? These were feelers sent out by the BSG team to determine our seriousness. When green lights were given all around, word got back to other IT staffers that we were serious after all. Many more suggestions surfaced. How about a business-oriented communication plan? Why don't we have a newsletter showing our successes and, more importantly, the successes of our clients? When these initiatives were green-lighted as well, momentum began to build.

As the service directory took shape, for example, IT service managers began to contact the BSG to ensure that their function was included and properly represented. Because of a small but growing sense of pride, no one wanted to be left out of this convenient, spiral-bound directory when it was printed in the thousands and distributed throughout all county government departments.

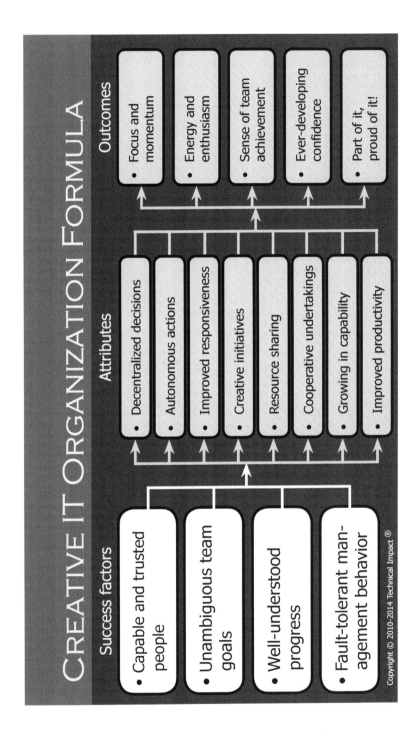

CREATIVE IT ORGANIZATION FORMULA

Success factors

- Capable and trusted people
- Unambiguous team goals
- Well-understood progress
- Fault-tolerant man- agement behavior

Attributes

- Decentralized decisions
- Autonomous actions
- Improved responsiveness
- Creative initiatives
- Resource sharing
- Cooperative undertakings
- Growing in capability
- Improved productivity

Outcomes

- Focus and momentum
- Energy and enthusiasm
- Sense of team achievement
- Ever-developing confidence
- Part of it, proud of it!

Various groups began describing desired performance outcomes with brief mantras. For computer operations, it was, "Lower than two seconds' response time, and no single point of failure." For applications development, it was, "As specified, on time and for the agreed price." We began to hear fewer complaints, a period we dubbed the "wait and see time." Then, instead of having to gauge our success on the basis of the relative silence, we started to receive actual kudos. With that, a spirit of competition among the various IT functions set in, and the trend was irreversible.

Meanwhile, we held a series of meetings with the client agencies to demonstrate that we understood their issues. About ten months in, the county librarian called. She had heard some good things about what we were doing and was considering "recentralizing" her data processing operation. Decentralization had come with its own headaches—IT staff were hard to retain, for example, because they had no career path in her department. She ended up signing back on with central IT, a move that we highlighted in our newsletter with her photo and the quote, "I don't know why I waited so long."

As others followed, central IT's billings grew dramatically. Over the next eighteen months, the unit costs for IT services fell to a point lower than it had been in years. More importantly, a good chunk of our IT professionals were demonstrating pride in their work, and creative ideas were flowing.

What I Learned

"Empowerment" is one of those terms that are so overused that they don't keep our attention for very long. Instead of employing it, I would sum up the lesson of this experience this way: Managers are served very well when they work to provide an environment where creativity can routinely happen.

What are the elements of such an environment? I believe only four basic things need to be in place:

- Employees who have the right skills and experience for their jobs and whom you have invested in and trained so that they feel respected and know that you trust them.
- A clear and unambiguous goal.
- Accurate and timely information that is routinely provided to employees so they know where they stand with respect to attaining their goals.
- A fault-tolerant standard of behavior at all management levels.

Each of these elements is important, but the last one is key. You will see no creativity from your employees unless they know with certainty that mistakes are not fatal to careers. They need to feel safe and know there is little or no risk associated with being creative. In fact, a mistake made by a trusted and experienced employee who has taken initiative on behalf of a client's need can be invaluable when the situation's lesson is openly shared.

I've also found that creative organizations are more flexible, move much faster and are much more competitive. When decisions for action can be made at the lowest levels of the management hierarchy, the client isn't forgotten and things happen a lot more responsively on their behalf.

Some in upper management fear this kind of environment and are loath to let go of any amount of power. Their knowledge and insight got them where they are, so surely they are the ones best qualified to make all decisions. To them, I'd like to pose two questions:

1. Would you rather be served by an autocratic or a creative organization?
2. Which would you rather work in?

After all, one way of looking at leadership was expressed by Mahatma Gandhi, who once pointed to a crowd and said, "There go my people; I must catch them, for I am their leader."

CHAPTER 16

Merry Widow in the Land of Milk & Honey: An Acquisition Disaster

> *Acquisition due diligence should include an in-depth IT assessment as a matter of course. So what were we thinking when we left IT on the sidelines as we set about acquiring a technology-based company?*

You would think that the people charged with conducting due diligence for a potential acquisition would subscribe to the adage, "Haste makes waste." Long ago, I was involved in an acquisition in which that saying was ignored, at great expense. It's a situation that's painful to recall but full of valuable lessons.

The target was a technology-based company. Its business involved receiving timely financial data over its own network, using proprietary software to analyze it and then providing the results to subscribers, again over its own network. The company's revenue stream was one hundred percent dependent on properly functioning IT.

Despite that, my technology function was not represented on the "acquisition hit team," as its members referred to it. I argued that my group's assessment could be crucial in such an acquisition, but the hit team's leader, an outside M&A

consultant, replied that it wouldn't be necessary because he was comfortable with technical matters. He told me that he didn't have time to keep every internal technical, corporate and administrative function involved in every acquisition decision. I was a newly appointed CIO, and seeing no support for my position, I didn't press the matter.

Very quickly, though, what should have been clear warnings about the dangerous ground we were treading on started appearing. To make sure that the acquisition was under the radar of the business community, the acquisition hit team gave the targeted company the code name of "Merry Widow." The team decided that the target should have a code name for referring to our company as well, and it thought it would be a sign of goodwill to let people at the target company choose one. Their response? "Milk and Honey." Somehow, no one on our team saw the significance in how Merry Widow pictured us.

Panic Sets In

A couple of weeks into due diligence, Merry Widow's financial and growth indicators looked positive. Its profitability appeared stable and rising, if slowly, and surprisingly, its costs didn't increase with volume growth or with recent additions to what was offered to Merry Widow's clients.

At that point, Merry Widow told the leader of our acquisition hit team that it had been approached by another company interested in acquiring it. Merry Widow's response had been "Not now," but our hit team leader panicked.

He convened an urgent meeting with our president and general management team (which included me). He told us that he and his team were very positive about Merry Widow, and therefore not surprised that another company was sniffing around. Because of the risk that we could lose the chance to acquire Merry Widow to a competitor, he suggested cutting the due diligence period from ninety days to thirty—two more weeks! A couple of us on the management team wanted to take longer and err on the side of caution. We argued that we needed to fully understand this technology-based company before investing in it. A compromise was reached: The due diligence period was cut to six weeks. Merry Widow quickly agreed. Another clue. . .

The rush to glory became unstoppable. Due diligence was completed early. Offers were made and exchanged. Merry Widow rejected our "earn-out periods" for key people; the owners of Merry Widow wanted their equity promptly, not drawn out over several years. Besides, another party was interested in acquiring them. Yet another clue, also ignored.

Finally, after a modest sum was set aside to deal with the cost of Merry Widow's integration, the acquisition was made, with some celebration.

Things unraveled fast from that point onward. Within a month, the two founders of Merry Widow and its CIO resigned. A senior manager from our company who was familiar with technology was quickly appointed as CEO of Merry Widow, and he soon became cognizant of the extent of Merry Widow client complaints. More Merry Widow staffers resigned.

Shortly after that, operational issues surfaced as some subscribers complained that they were not receiving any services. At that point, Merry Widow's appointed CEO called in the cavalry from the parent company and asked for an emergency assessment of Merry Widow's IT situation.

It was when my team finally arrived on the scene that the ugliness of the situation became fully clear.

We tried to learn what we could, but technical staffers were practically rushing out the door by this time. Merry

ACQUISITIONS WITHOUT IT SURPRISES

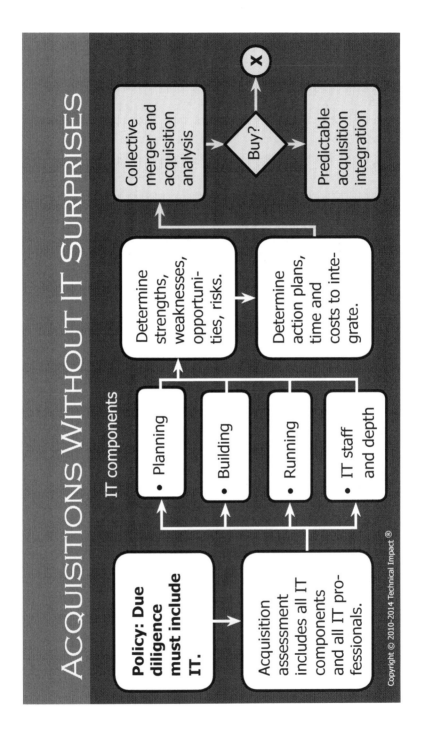

IT components

Policy: Due diligence must include IT.

Acquisition assessment includes all IT components and all IT professionals.

- Planning
- Building
- Running
- IT staff and depth

Determine strengths, weaknesses, opportunities, risks.

Determine action plans, time and costs to integrate.

Collective merger and acquisition analysis

Buy?

X

Predictable acquisition integration

Widow's chief systems engineer had taken a leave of absence, and the CIO was long gone. With no one to ask, my staff and I looked at what was left. We found seven months of trouble tickets and changes that had been requested by clients, with no action taken. The network had no redundancy built in, so network failures required all hands on deck. But all that could be done was to apply Band-Aids and wait for the next crisis. The processing capacity was severely underdeveloped and could not be increased without major expense. (At long last, we could understand why expansion had not resulted in significant cost increases.) For many months, the technical staff had been summoned to work through every weekend. IT staffers, burnt out from dealing with crisis after crisis, were resigning too fast to allow for their effective replacement. And since the people who originally developed Merry Widow's proprietary software were no longer around, there was no one left who knew what it did.

Merry Widow's newly appointed CEO wanted to know, "What will it take to fix it?"

The simple answer was that there was no overall fix. Some improvements were possible that would allow Merry Widow to maintain operations and customer service for a short time. The real problem was the proprietary software. It was no longer meeting clients' needs, but it could not be changed, maintained or reverse-engineered.

At another emergency session with the executive committee, Merry Widow's CEO summarized things, deferring to me on any questions about the state of the IT environment.

Painful as it was, it was agreed that we had transferred significant financial resources to others based upon an incomplete understanding of what we would receive in return. In the end, it was decided to remedy those short-term things that could be remedied and to disengage Merry Widow's clients (adding no new ones) in the most harmonious way possible. After about a year, Merry Widow no longer existed.

It was a hard lesson, but it was one we applied ever afterward. Other acquisitions were explored in the years that followed, and those that were completed were successful. Plenty of times, we found ourselves dealing with forthright, responsible management teams on the target company side, but we were always prepared to find out something else and gave ourselves every chance to discover the worst. One way we did this was to always include the IT function in the acquisition team. There were no more surprises.

Of the many takeaways from this experience for IT managers, I would emphasize the need to formalize your concerns. If you are an IT manager and you see risk, document it. It may not be in your position's description, but you have a responsibility to protect the stockholders' interests. Speak up, framing your concerns with an introduction such as, "I'd like to be clear on how the decisions we're making on this issue would avoid cost, improve service or increase revenue." You'd be surprised how such input can focus the discussion and keep it on point, especially if you are a stockholder as well.

Fools Rush In

The truth is, rushed acquisitions are not rare. As a matter of fact, over the past twenty-five years as a consultant and senior IT manager, it's scary how often I've seen such rushed processes. The IT discoveries come too late, and still it happens. I eventually created the term "integratibility" to help general management understand that it is essential that the targeted company's IT function be carefully considered during due diligence. The best outcome of such an assessment is that the IT environment is found to be reliable, reasonably compatible and well maintained and to have adequate capacity for the near future. Any other outcome needs to be fully addressed before completing the merger or moving on.

I wouldn't wish a Merry Widow on anyone. But even if you should encounter one, you can still deal with it constructively if the assessment is thorough and deliberate and includes IT.

If You Want to Land the Right Position, Ask the Right Questions

> *And if your questions elicit "the look," run away from that job as politely as possible.*

My first clue that the job I was interviewing for could be something special was the absence of "the look."

"The look" is my term for the facial expression we've all seen when we've asked someone something they just weren't prepared to answer. People who have the look don't want to seem surprised, dumbfounded or impolite, but they do want to buy a little time. They seem to make direct eye contact with you, but you can tell that their mental focus is somewhere else. Usually what has their full attention is an urgent internal search for some cogent words that will seem responsive to this question that they never thought they would receive. The look is not accompanied by words, though you may hear some "hmm's" and "uh's." There is also no nodding that would indicate "yes," and no head-shaking to indicate "no." Some variations include letting the mouth hang open slightly or tilting the head a few degrees. Even with these variables, however, the look is unmistakable.

I first noticed the look when I was a university instructor asking a question that a student wasn't prepared for. Later, as a manager, I'd see the look from time to time on the faces of my employees. One time, I even saw it briefly when I asked my wife's parents for their daughter's hand in marriage. That last example demonstrates that seeing the look isn't always a bad thing, since that turned out wonderfully for me. But my advice to anyone who sees it when they are interviewing for a job is to run.

Before I tell you about that job interview where my questions didn't elicit the look, I should tell you something about my earlier experiences in job interviews. Early on in my career, I had, "the disease to please," and wasn't too critical about the conditions surrounding the prospective position. I saw job interviews as my chance to find out how I could help the prospective employer and to communicate my eagerness to do that. If I got the job I interviewed for, I had the nice feeling that the company wanted me, and I was happy—for a while.

A few early positions turned out to be very different than the impression I'd received during the interview. Sure, some of those differences were positive, but most were negative, and in big ways. Clearly, my expectations weren't lined up properly with the day-in and day-out reality of the job. I can see now that this was mostly my fault. During the interview, I didn't particularly want to uncover things that didn't fit my idealized version of what I would be doing for the prospective employer.

It was slow in coming, but it finally dawned on me that it wasn't enough that a prospective company wanted me. Not even close, actually, if I wanted a better match to my expectations. I had to ask some probing questions during the interview. And if any of those questions prompted the look, I'd run, or at least get out as quickly as possible without sacrificing politeness and professionalism.

Eventually, my career had progressed to the point that I was interviewing with CEOs, chairmen and general managers of large enterprises for senior IT management positions. By then, I had learned to focus on the things that were most important to me, and so I would set out to determine the general management's view of IT's contribution to the enterprise. When it was my turn to ask questions, I might come at my issue by asking, "How does IT fit into your business strategy?" or "How does IT help the firm avoid cost, improve service and increase revenue?" or "Do you have a strategic goal in mind for IT and its value proposition to the enterprise?"

As if getting the look in response to any of these questions weren't bad enough, I would sometimes even hear things like, "We don't look at IT that way" or "IT is a necessary evil. It's techies with their toys talking jargon and not understanding the business that pays their salaries" or "They don't know their place. We need someone who will whip them into shape."

Of course, I didn't always feel like running out of an interview. After all, if I was going to insist that my questions not be met by the look, that insistence had to be reasonable, or I would never work in IT again.

One time in an interview, I asked a board chairman, "How do you see the distributed systems environment fitting into your business strategy?"

This gentleman didn't give me the look at all. He didn't even miss a beat before responding that distributed systems were very important to his strategy because he wanted his employees to have better access to critical information so

TARGETING YOUR IT PROGRESS

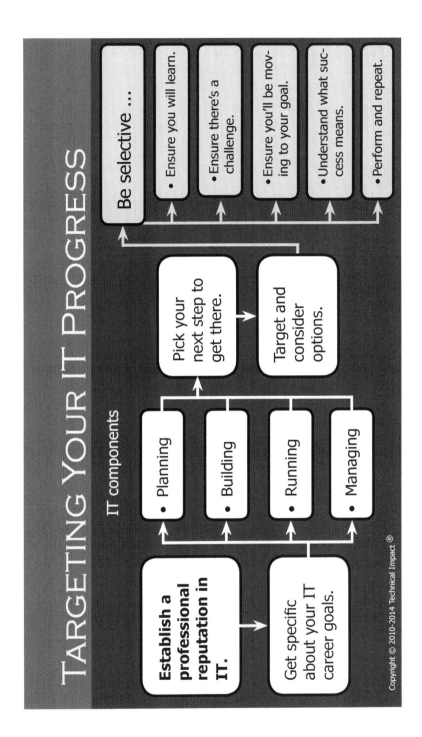

IT components

Establish a professional reputation in IT.

Get specific about your IT career goals.

- Planning
- Building
- Running
- Managing

Pick your next step to get there.

Target and consider options.

Be selective …

- Ensure you will learn.
- Ensure there's a challenge.
- Ensure you'll be moving to your goal.
- Understand what success means.
- Perform and repeat.

that they could make the most effective business decisions possible and therefore simplify customer interactions.

To which I probably smiled and nodded. But inside, I was shouting, "Wow!"

He wasn't done. "Think about it," he said. "Our employees get defensive in front of our customers if they can't responsively get access to the information they need to properly serve them. If that happens, our customers start to roll their eyes. That's the exact opposite of the situation we need to establish with our distributed systems function."

Then he hooked me. He said, "Distributed systems are a critical link in allowing our employees to respond quickly and creatively to our client needs. Why? Simply because an effective distributed systems environment integrates local data with a pull-down of centralized information from many sources. If we want to move fast as a business, we must allow as many decisions as possible to be made at the edge of the enterprise. 'Empowerment' is an overused word these days, but the last thing we need is to have every decision go up to some central point and back down just so everyone's backside is covered. That's bureaucratic and glacially slow. Our folks can be creative and responsive only if they have an environment that allows them to be, and our customers will sense this, and our business will grow."

I was hooked because he used the word "creative" to describe what he wanted employees at the edge of the business to be. I already knew that this is one of the most powerful energy releasers there is.

I was on board within sixty days. Over several years, I was able to assist the chairman and his general management team achieve the decentralized decision-making environment they had jointly committed to. While it took some time and their continued support, their goal was eventually realized for each business in the enterprise.

My expectations? Exceeded. My contributions were the ones I wanted to make, and they were supported and consistently recognized for their benefits to the enterprise. My sense of accomplishment and reward in that position was the highest in my career.

It took me a while to find it, though, and it didn't exactly happen by accident.

Years later, I heard Lily Tomlin say something that would have served as great career advice in my early years: "When I was young, I made up my mind that I would grow up to be somebody. Now, I wish I'd been more specific."

CHAPTER 18

There's No Lasting Change Without Buy-in

> *Of course, you can always leave things exactly the way they are—for a while.*

It was about the rockiest start to a major IT initiative I've ever been involved in. Because I'd implemented IT marketing programs (now called client relationship management, or CRM) earlier in my career, the CIO charged me with doing the same for his organization.

Of course, projects that sail along smoothly, with no resistance, are great. But it's the ones that throw lots of roadblocks in our way that end up teaching us things.

We were in trouble from the start. In a meeting with all of his direct reports (which included me), the CIO declared his intention to establish a CRM program. He didn't offer any reasons for this. He just announced that I would be directing the effort and stated that he expected everyone's full cooperation. My peers were mostly silent, but I could feel the tension in the room. A few comments were made that made it clear why this initiative was receiving such a cold reaction.

The one that best summed things up: "We're up to our necks in work, and we're now supposed to pony up resources and time to create whatever CRM is?"

I said that I would be answering the question of "whatever CRM is" at a meeting in a few days. I didn't sense much enthusiasm for that, either.

In the days that followed, several fellow IT managers called to ask about this "CRM thing." Most of them implied that we didn't need it at all. The more accommodating said it could wait until next year.

Negotiating Buy-in

I could understand why some of my fellow managers might be panicking. We all had more than we could do already. Any new initiative was bound to sound like just another thing that we couldn't give the proper attention to.

It's been my experience that change can't be mandated. For it to really take hold and transform an organization, you need buy-in. Tell a group of people that you plan to make some major changes in the way things are done, and the thought going through the head of each and every one of them will be, What's in it for me? We hadn't even attempted to answer that question yet, and as the days passed, there was nothing to stop the resistance from growing.

Winning buy-in from stakeholders can be tricky in the best of circumstances, but I had a taller wall to scale than normal, simply because there had been time for rumor and misinformation to foster discontent. I wasn't sure how to overcome the resistance that was building at my upcoming meeting, so I talked to another IT manager. She didn't hesitate. Her advice was to show our peers what happens in an IT organization that doesn't have a CRM program and then show how things work in an IT organization with a mature

CRM program in place. Then, she said, "explain the differences and ask us which one we'd rather be." It was a brilliant idea.

I prepared my material, scheduled the meeting and informed everyone that I would identify the pros and cons of CRM programs. In an effort to ensure attendance, I said that each manager would be expected to tell me what they thought CRM would mean for their part of the IT organization—in other words, they would be asked to vote.

At the meeting, I began by saying that, whether we had a CRM program or not, we should view our IT service organization as a business and ourselves as its owners. While IT wasn't itself a profit center, the decisions we made affected the costs of our clients on the business side. We had to seriously consider that our clients viewed outside IT service firms as our competition.

"So, CRM will help us prove we're the best alternative?" one manager asked.

"It will," I said, "but I don't expect you to take my word for it. Let me show you instead."

I then laid out what defined us now, as an IT service organization with no CRM program in place:

1. We don't have any formal marketing sense about our clients.
2. We don't know what services they use, what they're happy and unhappy with, what their measures of success are, what their billings are, who the IT decision-makers are, what their IT usage profile is (by line of business) or what our role is or is supposed to be in supporting their success and managing their risk.
3. Clients and even other parts of IT service

don't know how to best obtain our services.

4. We don't have any repeatable way to make sure we have the resources needed and in place to honor every commitment we make. We tend to promise things and then try to figure out what's required later.

5. We don't have any cross-functional management or coordination capability—we react.

6. We lack a consistent notion of how to create and add value to each business we serve.

7. We don't manage the expectations of our clients with a comprehensive description of our services.

8. We don't appropriately capture revenue for all services, and our billing can be unpredictable.

9. We sometimes blame other parts of our own organization for a missed commitment, giving clients the impression that IT is a dysfunctional organization.

10. We don't share our direction and strategy with our clients or seek feedback on how we could be more responsive.

The CIO then called for discussion on these characteristics. Several managers were defensive at first, but the CIO was able to draw out a general acknowledgment that by really owning our service organization, we could begin to address each of these undesirable traits.

That was my cue to move on to the characteristics of an IT service organization with a mature CRM program in place:

1. It has a service directory that's written in client terms and is available as a hard copy and

online.

2. It makes integrated bids on projects, with each IT service aspect represented as needed, and all coordinated through an account relationship management function.

3. It reviews service-level commitments for continuous improvement opportunities.

4. It proactively deals with client issues.

5. It has a formal marketing plan for each business and function it supports.

6. It routinely communicates with clients in multiple ways, touting accomplishments, heralding direction, highlighting client success and soliciting feedback.

7. Its intra-service coordination is seamless, and performance is consistently excellent.

8. Each IT service line of business is benchmarked annually to show performance and cost differentials compared with external alternatives.

9. Clients routinely ask for IT's advice on using recently developed technologies to avoid cost, improve their client services and increase their revenue.

10. Clients clearly appreciate IT's value and its services to them and see it as a powerful ally and involved partner in achieving their business goals.

Which One Should We Be?

Now the managers had two sharply differentiated organizational profiles to consider. What, the CIO wanted to know, were the pros and cons of each? The single advantage of stay-

COMMERCIALIZING THE IT FUNCTION

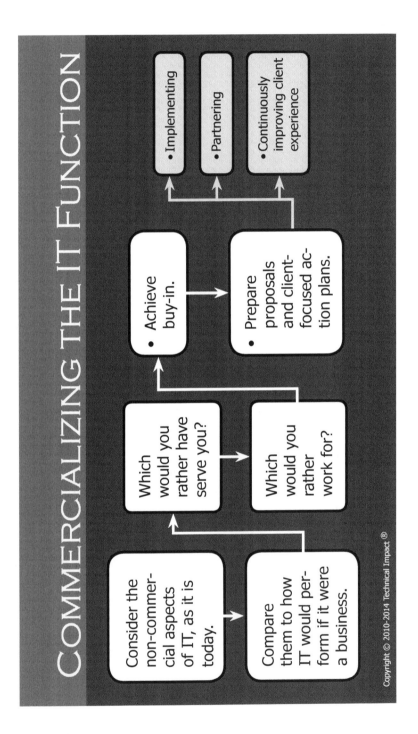

- Consider the non-commercial aspects of IT, as it is today.

- Compare them to how IT would perform if it were a business.

- Which would you rather have serve you?

- Which would you rather work for?

- Achieve buy-in.

- Prepare proposals and client-focused action plans.

- Implementing

- Partnering

- Continuously improving client experience

ing as we were was simply that it was the easiest option—in the short term. The cons were that clients went without information and were unhappy, that employees were frustrated, that clients felt that outsourcing would be preferable and that, despite knowing about our problems, we had done nothing about them.

On the plus side for changing were some simple facts: Our clients' experience with our IT service would improve dramatically, as would IT employees' understanding of their role in providing it, and IT service would improve. The only con we could think of was that until benchmarking was done, clients might see the CRM function as bureaucratic or an additional expense.

Then I made the choice more stark by posing two questions:

- Which IT service organization would you rather have serve you?
- Which would you rather work for?

In the end, we had our buy-in; the entire management team fully endorsed the idea of CRM implementation.

As we moved on to execution of the plan, we staffed the CRM team with people proficient in interpersonal communications and consultative skills, and then we kept them focused on critical CRM processes. The client-focused transformation, once begun, was irreversible. Benchmarks gave us a basis for competitive comparisons and continued improvement. Service directory information was in demand the minute it became available. CRM gave rise to outside training initiatives, including industry best practices, for all IT professional staff. IT professionals started to feel more respected and proud of their contribution and value to the enterprise.

As for the "What's in it for me?" question, it gradually answered itself as our desired outcomes began to be achieved. It took a while, but our constant state of reaction was gradually replaced as more time became available to us and we were able to more favorably influence our future. Strategic discussions, previously rare (given the fact that our beepers would never shut up), became routine.

By the way, a key aspect of the CRM unit's communication plan urged the entire management team to get out of our offices much more often to meet with both clients and staff. It was an undeniably good idea, so we all agreed. And guess what. The CRM unit began tracking us to make sure we followed through.

'The Techies Are Going to Tell Me How to Make Money?'

> *If you think you can learn and grow while you remain inside your comfort zone, see what happens when you get out of it once in a while.*

I think I choked.

I was the senior IT manager in a meeting called by the CEO of the leaders of our various lines of business. Since his arrival, this CEO had shown himself to be a visionary. He had made IT his focus, directing us to fix broken and outdated financial and operational support systems. Now, high above Manhattan, he laid out his plans for where to go from there. IT would again be central, but in a role entirely new to it. That's where I choked.

The CEO began by reviewing our progress. Costs were down, and customer service was showing improvement. All well and good, he said, but now we needed to turn our attention in another direction, urgently. With costs already cut, it was time to focus on increasing revenue. "I called this meeting because I've decided that IT must take the initiative and lead this new effort from now on, and I wanted you to prepare yourselves accordingly."

IT would lead a drive to increase revenue? Nothing in my experience had prepared me for a statement like that, much less the reality of leading such an effort. But the CEO was continuing, explaining that a company whose main product was information had to develop electronic means of delivering that product if it was going to survive. Unfortunately, he said, the company's business leaders "just aren't aware of what's going on in technology. So how can they be expected to exploit it to increase their revenue?"

He finished by laying down a clear challenge to IT: Give him a plan whereby IT would collaborate with each line of business to develop new, profitable electronically based products over the next year. "Just tell me what you need," he said in closing.

Later, alone in my car while driving back to my office in the suburbs, I was in mental turmoil. I wasn't too bad at planning, building and running IT systems and services, but I'd never done a full business plan, and I honestly didn't know in detail how each line of business that used my services made money. And I was supposed to know what their clients would want in the future?

I eventually calmed down when it dawned on me that the CEO's challenge was exactly what the IT team needed in order for it to be a powerful ally and involved partner. This was going to take a lot of work, sure, but the more I thought about it, the more I saw that we would learn a great deal. And some of it might even be fun.

Learn we did, and the first lesson for me (see box) concerned what constitutes real leadership.

We're in Charge

After some fits and starts, the CEO created a new product

Lessons Learned

The lessons I drew from this experience have certainly stood the test of time:

1. Leadership means introducing beneficial change. (That's what the CEO did, even if it meant leaving his charges feeling uncomfortable and dealing with complexity.)

2. People support best what they help build, and that makes buy-in possible. (We wrote our own charter—how could we argue with it?)

3. Direct answers to simple business questions are always best (especially if the questions are exactly what the stockholder would ask).

4. The IT organization has to display real business acumen and show an awareness of what matters to the business side. (The days when IT could be a reactive bystander to what goes on in the enterprise are over.)

5. Lasting change always arrives on a path of awareness, trial, adaptation and adoption. (The most important step is gaining awareness, and this happens to be everyone's ongoing job.)

6. The IT organization must represent itself as a powerful marketing ally to the businesses it supports (which it really is).

development group (PDG) made up of key marketing and sales professionals from each line of business in the corporation, as well as myself and a senior strategy director.

IT AS A PARTNER IN NEW BUSINESS GROWTH

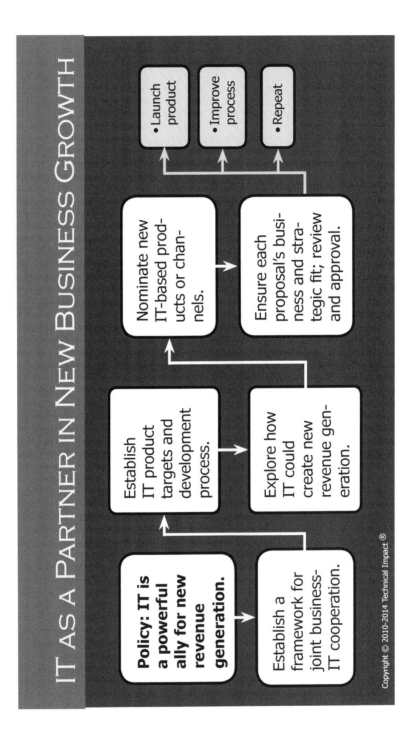

Policy: IT is a powerful ally for new revenue generation.

Establish a framework for joint business-IT cooperation.

Establish IT product targets and development process.

Explore how IT could create new revenue generation.

Nominate new IT-based products or channels.

Ensure each proposal's business and strategic fit; review and approval.

- Launch product
- Improve process
- Repeat

We would write our own charter, the CEO told us. Before he parted, he added, "I need your charter and plan of action in two weeks."

A deadline like that can really give you focus. We didn't ramble much, and the resulting PDG charter was simple. Each line of business would identify three new electronically based products or services within the next six months, and those that won approval for development would be in the marketplace within twelve months. Working together on that charter delivered my second lesson. (See "Lessons Learned" box.)

Next, with very welcome outside help from Schrello and Associates, we used three questions that would help us identify potential electronically based products:

1. **Is it real?** Is the market real? Is there a need for the product or service? Is there a clear idea for the product or service? Can it be provided? Will customers buy it?

2. **Can we win?** Can our offering be competitive in its features, promotion, price and timing? Can our company be competitive in its marketing, sales and management?

3. **Is it worth it?** Will it be profitable? Can we afford it? Is the return/risk acceptable? Does it satisfy other needs or build other relationships useful to our future?

Oversimplified, sure, but we figured that if we couldn't answer the questions a stockholder would ask, we'd never get any of our ideas funded for development, much less assure that they would be successful in the marketplace. We also reasoned that our credibility would be very short-lived if we didn't have these answers nailed down. (See "Lessons Learned" box for Lesson No. 3.)

That brought us to the hard part: getting each line of business to the point where it would consider creating and trying to develop new electronically based products. Someone in the group pointed out that people will never try something new if they aren't aware of it in the first place.

With that thought in mind, we set out to understand each line of business's customer acquisition and retention cycles and then to inform the business managers about how IT could help them avoid cost, improve service and increase revenue. We had expected it to be tough to educate them about the possibilities of electronic delivery of information products, since they were pretty much clueless about technology. But we were helped out when our competition began to bring out such products. With no prompting from us, the business managers were saying things like, "If they can do that, why can't we?"

It wasn't long before we realized that in most cases the data, knowledge and wisdom embodied in our traditionally published products was already stored electronically. Repurposing this information was not technically difficult, and offering it electronically eventually became very profitable indeed.

As for the fun part? This challenging time had more than its share of pressure, but we all felt that we learned so much and felt so productive, it was well worth it. Not least of what we gained was the realization by both business managers and the IT community that by combining forces we could achieve much more than if we approached our objectives separately.

So, after nearly choking at the prospect of getting in over my head, I had one of the most rewarding experiences of my professional career. That, of course, is no mere coincidence.

CHAPTER 20

A Measure of Success

> *Even if IT is improving efficiency, is it aligned with the business's goals?*

As the executive who had recruited the company's CIO, the COO had reason to be proud of the improvements that had been made to the IT function. And he was. But this COO had a larger vision than most, and so it was that I, a senior IT management consultant, had come to be sitting in his office, listening to him say, "I have a problem, and I'd like to know how it can be solved."

He continued, "We've invested heavily in our IT function, and I'm proud of its efficiency improvements. I selected our CIO because he knew exactly how to convert our undisciplined IT function into what we have today."

Nonetheless, he felt it was necessary to go beyond those efficiency improvements. "As I look at our competition, I can see that an efficient IT function is just for openers. They're using new technologies better than we are, and they're outpacing us. The market is changing faster than we are. We need better intelligence, and we need IT to accelerate our strategic achievement, as a full partner."

Okay, I said, but why are you talking to me about this and not your CIO?

"I've tried, more than once," he said, with some exasperation. "It's become clear to me that we are continually talking past each other. I don't blame him. I'm partially responsible for this situation. But the bottom line is that he doesn't know how to convert my strategy into action, and I don't know what to tell him to do first."

As a former CIO myself, I was pleased to hear him say that he didn't believe that changing his CIO was the solution. He didn't want to replace him with someone who could address the issue of strategic direction while losing the momentum they had going in IT efficiency. That was where I came in: Someone who could work alongside the CIO and open his eyes to what the COO needed from him.

"Can you help?" he wanted to know.

"I believe I can," I said. "I need to understand the business and the situation better, so I'd like to see your formally declared strategy, your mission and the near-term goals of both the enterprise and all the business units within it. I also want to meet with the CIO to learn about all of the applications and system development efforts under way. And I'll need two weeks."

He seemed pleased, and intrigued. "Well," he said, "that's not a lot to ask for. What do you expect to accomplish?"

I told him that I suspected that there would be enough precision in the strategy, mission and near-term goals to build an IT investment framework that could be used to objectively measure strategic investment priorities and progress against current strategic goals.

"A framework?" he said. "I like the sound of that. This

could be just what we need." I could tell he was thinking things through, but at that point I didn't know enough about him to realize how far ahead of me he was.

Building the Framework

The meeting with the CIO went well. I'd sent him a list of what I was looking for and he was ready. His system development group had seven projects under way, four of them major and the result of several business units combining their resources to better address customer issues through IT.

Naturally, he wanted to know where all this was going, and I told him that the COO wanted to build on the efficiency of the IT function by providing a way to objectively measure IT progress on strategic issues. By way of reassurance, I added, "This will give you and your staff a better sense of your accomplishments for the business."

The formal business strategy material was specific enough that I could fairly easily extract four strategic imperatives that would lead to profitability and growth. *All of them could be improved through more effectively applied IT:*

1. Operational excellence
   - Operational focus on performance
   - Lowest effective cost results
   - Addressing all quality measures daily
2. Customer satisfaction
   - Quick, easy, accurate and pleasant transactions
   - Knowledgeable, responsive, hassle-free service
   - Individualized treatment/fulfillment
3. Positioning for future industry leadership
   - Better customer/competitive intelligence
   - New products, services, forms of delivery
   - Very rapid time to market

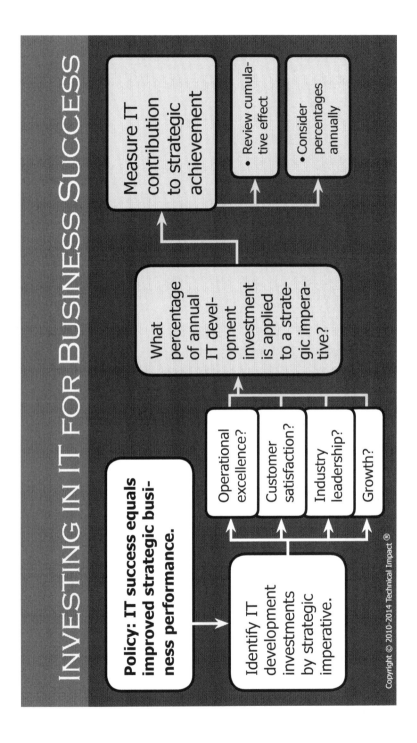

INVESTING IN IT FOR BUSINESS SUCCESS

Policy: IT success equals improved strategic business performance.

Identify IT development investments by strategic imperative.

- Operational excellence?
- Customer satisfaction?
- Industry leadership?
- Growth?

What percentage of annual IT development investment is applied to a strategic imperative?

Measure IT contribution to strategic achievement

- Review cumulative effect
- Consider percentages annually

- Global offerings with local adaptation
4. Responsiveness to change

With the CIO's help, I linked the planned IT projects to the relevant strategic goals. What I saw was that the COO was correct in his impression.

The two development projects aimed at optimizing internal administrative processes were directed solely toward Goal 1, operational excellence. Their outcomes were obviously desirable, but the efforts represented major investments yet wouldn't significantly improve innovation, business growth or profitability (Goals 2-4).

Four other projects were directed primarily toward Goal 2, customer satisfaction. They were a universal customer call center service support system, a data retrieval project for cost per call and quality per call, an integrated billing system and an air route optimization system. They were also clearly worthwhile, but while they would avoid cost and improve service, they would not significantly contribute to new revenues or growth (Goals 3 and 4).

The final project, a data warehouse, was a killer enabler for Goal 3, positioning for future industry leadership, and Goal 4, responsiveness to change. It was a major project, but it reflected only a small percentage of the enterprise's overall IT investment commitment. The bulk of IT investment was focused on operational excellence and customer satisfaction strategies, and not on growth. The breakdown of the IT development funding targets was: avoiding cost, thirty-eight percent; improving service, forty-four percent; and increasing revenue, eighteen percent.

Building on the Framework

When I brought the framework and my findings to the

COO, I began to perceive the subtlety of his mind. His analysis was thorough and lightning-quick, and he immediately saw the findings' implication that the IT function's leadership was not the sole cause of his situation.

He began by commenting, "One snapshot like this cannot possibly tell the whole story. We have to look at this framework at least every year, and cumulatively, to understand how sustained our direction is to our strategic achievement, both through IT and otherwise."

He went on: "This exercise has shown us that we'll need to work together with IT differently now. IT needs to come forth as a partner to share with each strategic business how technology is changing and how emerging technologies might be used to improve our productivity *and* increase our revenue. Business units will also need to annually come forth with new revenue-producing initiatives which could be enabled by more effective IT."

What he was saying reminded me of a quote from futurist Ray Kurzweil that I'm fond of: "The more intelligent process will inherently outcompete all others, making intelligence the most powerful force in the universe."

And my encounter with that uncommon COO left me with the realization that an essential priority for any enterprise is to continually improve its corporate intelligence with ever better information, knowledge and wisdom about its clients, its competition and its likely opportunities.

IT can be a powerful ally in making this happen.

The Case for Quality

> *For IT, close adherence to quality metrics ensures that it is doing what the business really needs it to do.*

Do you think that your life as an IT manager is stressful and intense? Try applying for a Malcolm Baldrige National Quality Award (NQA) and you'll know what real stress and intensity are.

That's a serious suggestion, though: Try applying for one. But only if you've done all the groundwork to really prepare you for the scrutiny you'll receive. It's doing the groundwork, and getting your organization aligned with the quality precepts on which the NQA is judged, that makes the entire process worthwhile. I guarantee that it will benefit your organization in profound ways.

My initial experience with the NQA was a bit unusual, but I think it does nonetheless demonstrate that IT quality initiatives have real payback.

I'd long been a CIO for various enterprises and institutions. Although IT service quality had always been a concern throughout my IT management career, I'd been unable to establish a definition of it that I was happy with. Sure, I had some general guidelines for overall results. For example, I summed up optimal network performance as "always available, with no single point of failure." For computer services: "always available, response times of two seconds or less." For application development: "on time, as specified and at the agreed cost."

As for more in-depth quality measures, well, the works of Deming and Crosby were enlightening, but their principles were meant for the reduction of defects in products. Cross-walking them to the reduction of IT service failures usually left me with more questions than answers.

Then I joined a start-up business, and all that changed. The CEO made it clear that he had something very different in mind for his new company and his CIO. His company would be organized, built and operated around the NQA performance measures. As for his CIO, efficient IT service delivery would be required. More importantly, though, I would have the responsibility of ensuring that every business function in the firm had the information it needed to make ever better decisions for the customer, and to make them ever quicker.

While I was still interviewing, the CEO asked me if I'd ever done this kind of thing before. No, I told him. "Do you know how to do it?" "Not yet." I must have sounded ready and willing to learn, because he hired me.

But what had I gotten myself into? I was used to being responsible for the delivery of IT services, but now I would be judged on how well the business performed using the information that my function provided. That information had to be effective in terms of improving the strategic performance of the business.

What made the job irresistible to me was the chance to come into a company with no installed base. I would be building the IT function from the ground up. What IT manager wouldn't jump at a chance like that? On the other hand, I would have to make the IT function truly and measurably effective upon business launch.

Step by Step

The effects of the CEO's directive to me were felt immediately as my application systems development professionals and I started to set up shop. Given my very clear mandate to assist the business in achieving its strategic goals, we couldn't just say, "We need this, this and this. Authorize our purchases, please." Instead, we met with each business component to establish their information needs. Then we created a diagram of the overall flow of essential information for the entire business and each component within it. After this, we revised and verified our findings with each business component. Next, I presented the flow diagram to the senior executive committee. With interim approval from the SEC, the next step was to work together with each business component in preparing one-page business cases for the IT investments that would be needed to meet the flow requirements. Finally, each of those was presented to the SEC, which then approved and prioritized them in keeping with the pace allowed for IT investment.

Upon completion of that process, we were ready to start the IT infrastructure and systems development. While that work was quite typical for getting a business off the ground, there was something about it that was very different for me. Because of all the back-and-forth with the business units that had preceded this phase, I knew precisely, for the first time in my career, how the business made its profit and in what ways the IT function's performance was a factor in generating client satisfaction, growth and profitability.

For example, the marketing function needed timely intelligence on client prospects and competition. It needed the ability to make projections based upon different decision sets so that it could introduce timely and profitable product variations. It needed to gather early specifics of trends and the always-changing customer satisfiers regarding our products, to ensure that if they changed, we could change quickly in response.

And the operations function needed data on incoming client calls so that they could be routed to the service agent who was most familiar with the client or who spoke the appropriate language. The call would also populate the service agent's display with the latest information on the client. Calls would be handled quickly and efficiently because all the relevant information the agent needed would be on-screen as the call was answered.

The Quality Factor

Under the program envisioned by the CEO, all of that was just the beginning when it came to quality. We had a quality oversight group that reported to the CEO, and it got around to us just as the IT function was about to go into its operational readiness phase. Marketing research had led this group to develop nine categories of customer satisfaction and about thirty secondary satisfiers, and it was now visiting the various business components to determine the things the business units did that affected those satisfiers. When something was identified as having a positive effect on the satisfiers, it became a quality metric, closely associated with ensuring that satisfaction levels were achieved or exceeded. The IT function ended up with sixty-five quality metrics that

IT DELIGHTING CUSTOMERS = IT QUALITY

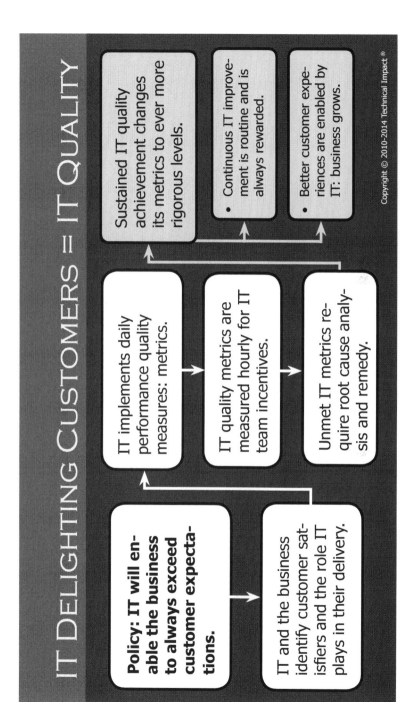

Policy: IT will enable the business to always exceed customer expectations.

IT and the business identify customer satisfiers and the role IT plays in their delivery.

IT implements daily performance quality measures: metrics.

IT quality metrics are measured hourly for IT team incentives.

Unmet IT metrics require root cause analysis and remedy.

Sustained IT quality achievement changes its metrics to ever more rigorous levels.

- Continuous IT improvement is routine and is always rewarded.

- Better customer experiences are enabled by IT: business grows.

we assiduously monitored from that point on. Over half of these metrics addressed IT delivery, and the rest had to do with IT's effective performance in support of business components.

The NQA criteria even extended to team performance measures and compensation, and this was very important in making the whole structure work. Throughout the company, regardless of management level, base salary was augmented by a quality bonus that was based solely on the percentage of quality measures hit or exceeded on a daily basis. Believe me, it was a pleasure to see how this incentive led to everyone helping each other. When a metric was missed, we jointly tried and determine the root cause.

Continuous improvement was also baked in. When a metric was attained two months in a row, its performance requirement was increased, either by reducing its cycle time or adding more to be accomplished in the same cycle time.

Three Years Later

The senior examiner leading the NQA review team during a site visit to our firm took me aside and told me that he and his staff would need to know a few things: "Since the inception of your business, how many customers have you gained? How many customers have you lost? And what have you done about these facts in each case?" Then he added, "Of course, we'll need to see the detailed evidence for each of your responses."

I did in fact know the answers to these questions. Not because of any special effort on my part, but because it was built in to our processes from the beginning.

Thanks primarily to our CEO's foresight, we were awarded the Malcolm Baldrige NQA in the Service category that year. And the company reached profitability two years earlier than was expected in the business plan. It's hard for me to think that those two facts have nothing to do with each other.

I know that this instance was extraordinary in that the IT function was built from scratch with a moderate but still exceptional IT investment pace. That just makes everything easier; as the old joke goes: "God may have created the world in seven days, but he didn't have an installed base." But I've seen many similar best practice approaches implemented very effectively and with exceptional results, regardless of the scale, nature or age of the installed base.

If you were to ask me whether a business case can be made for IT quality initiatives around avoiding cost, improving service and increasing revenue, I would have to say that the evidence is compelling.

Finance Matters

> In fact, it matters a lot.
> IT leaders need to under-
> stand this and arm them-
> selves with a methodology
> that lets them demon-
> strate how IT investments
> will improve business
> performance.

I've made it pretty clear in other chapters how essential it is for IT leaders to communicate with the enterprise's business leaders. It's how we know what direction to move with our resources and where investment is needed.

Imagine, then, how disconcerting it was for me to be placed in a position of determining my budget needs without consulting with my business peers. I quickly found that I couldn't do what I had been asked to do. But that problem was straightened out soon enough, and after it was, I found myself communicating very beneficially with the company's CFO. What I learned from her during that budget season stayed with me for the rest of my career.

It all began in a year of flat profits and no growth. The CEO decided to do away with incremental budgeting in favor of zero-based budgeting. That meant we had to justify every penny we proposed spending, and not just the increases over the previous year.

Every member of the senior management committee (SMC) was told to prepare for a meeting by compiling two lists, one tallying those things that were necessary to keep the company functioning at a bare-bones level, the other listing things deemed "nice to have," at least in our independent judgment.

And that was the problem. As the senior IT manager in the company, I had prepared my two lists, but we had all taken that "independent judgment" directive seriously, and it was a killer obstacle for me.

That was because every aspect of my IT services management function needed to grow, remain steady or shrink depending on the needs of the various strategic business units and the collective capacity demands of the enterprise. In past budget preparations, I would meet with the manager of each strategic unit to assess client growth, transaction volume, equipment and software development needs, etc. Their input would let me match capacities and expenses to ensure that the IT function could remain reasonably responsive throughout the following fiscal year.

Absent the ability to collect that sort of information, my bare-bones list could only include projections of historical trends for existing operational systems and services, and no expenses for new ones. Anything other than historical projections would have to be justified, which I couldn't do alone. As for "nice to have" items, without any input from the business, these were directed solely at improving the IT function's productivity and services or to avoid cost. There was no way to assess new requirements on the IT function. Part of me was certain that this would change, but my dark side worried that if my numbers were adopted, the enterprise would be flying blind into the future. This budget process seemed incapable of avoiding a shortfall of IT capacity in some area during the coming year. If revenue was lost as a result, we would scramble to add the needed IT capacity, but that would take time, and more time would mean more lost revenue. That would be very bad for the enterprise and would reflect poorly on the IT function, regardless of my inability to make better projections because of the constraints of the budget process. The term *"career-limiting position"* rang in my head.

Collaboration Needed

I headed to the SMC meeting primed to make the case for collaboration in the budget process, but I was pleasantly surprised to discover that just about everyone else had had the same thought. As they presented their own budget projections, nearly every business unit SMC member suggested that more time be allotted to allow them and me to discuss their IT needs for the following year. They just couldn't figure out their IT needs for themselves.

The CEO wasn't happy about the delay, but he shouldered a share of the blame and told us to get to work so we could wrap things up at the next meeting. Then he put me on the spot by saying that, since IT was the reason for the delay, he expected me to come to the next meeting prepared to present a framework for IT investments. The CFO would be happy to help me if I needed it, he added.

If I needed it?

As I set to my task, I turned to the business case methodology, which I had relied on before. With it, I could evaluate the problems an investment was meant to address and assess how things would look if the investment were made compared to how they would be if the investment were not made. As a guiding principle, a business case had to be at least a little persuasive before further quantification was justified. And if the investment outcome was persuasive enough, the quantification would take the form of cost avoidance, service improvement and/or revenue increase, plus return on investment. I thought this method was nice and tidy, a good way to compare different ways of using investment funding to roughly establish priorities, based on return and how quickly investments could be implemented.

I used the business case methodology to run a couple of IT investments I had proposed in my initial stab at drawing up budget priorities. With it, I was able to make a decent case for things like a second diesel generator for backup, which I felt we needed in case the first one failed. In determining ROI, I calculated that if our generator did not come online after a power failure, revenue lost would exceed the cost to buy and install a second generator in under three minutes. Local power grid failures were common, and their average duration was over twenty-five minutes.

But I wanted a reality check, and so I went to see the CFO. She liked my approach as far as it went, but she was quick to spot its weaknesses. "You say the business case for an investment has to be persuasive to warrant further quantification," she noted. Now, define 'persuasive' for me. Or, let's come at this from another direction. How does your business case approach address the strategic performance value of an investment?"

Thank God for reality checks! The business case methodology didn't handle the strategic performance of an investment, which meant that investments made using it might not help the enterprise achieve its strategy one bit. Or worse, investment funding could actually be counterproductive to the strategic outcomes of the enterprise. Not a good way to spend money.

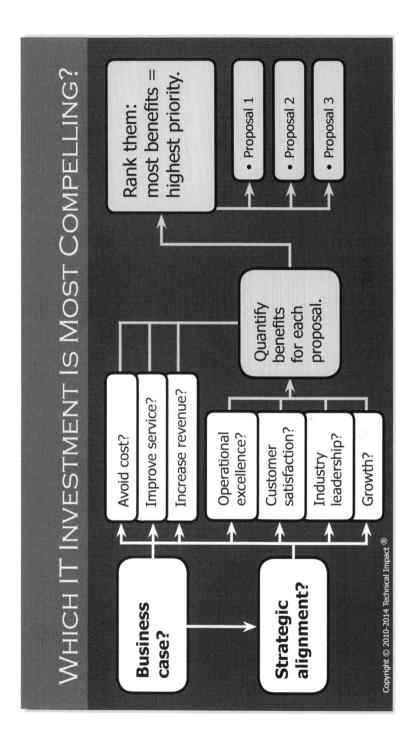

WHICH IT INVESTMENT IS MOST COMPELLING?

Rank them:
most benefits =
highest priority.

- Proposal 1
- Proposal 2
- Proposal 3

Quantify
benefits
for each
proposal.

Avoid cost?

Improve service?

Increase revenue?

Operational excellence?

Customer satisfaction?

Industry leadership?

Growth?

Business case?

Strategic alignment?

The CFO and I worked on this for a few days, and she hit on what turned out to be a brilliant but simple-to-understand strategic component to add to my rather tactical business case approach. She defined "persuasive" to mean an investment that met both the business case investment criteria *and* what she termed the strategic investment criteria.

First, she boiled down our enterprise's strategic goals (from our formal mission and strategic declaration materials) to four terms:

(a) Operational excellence
(b) Customer satisfaction
(c) Positioning for industry leadership
(d) Growth

Then we did the same with the business case objectives:

(1) Avoiding cost
(2) Improving service
(3) Increasing revenue
(4) ROI

Finally, we devised a grid with (a) to (d) as the horizontal rows and (1) to (4) as the vertical columns. If an investment was to be considered for funding, it had to have a value in at least one of the boxes making up the row/column intersections. The more boxes that were filled in on the grid and the higher the values, the more compelling any investment would be. It made sense.

We tried it out with some investment examples from my lists. My second diesel generator, for example, avoided cost and improved service in the operational excellence row, so it could be considered for funding against other investments and might finally win favor if the values were high enough. A second example, repaving the parking lot, would provide an ROI, but it would take forever to do so, and it wasn't an urgent need. While it could be argued that it would avoid cost, there was no strategic goal you could apply it to. Should such an investment compete with a second diesel generator investment? No way.

The CFO presented these investment criteria at the next SMC session. It was immediately accepted and, with some minor tweaking, it has been used ever since.

And when it was my time to relate to the CEO and the SMC what the IT function would need in the following year, I was more than ready.

CHAPTER 23

Directing Discovery

> *There's no stopping change, but you can influence and lead it by continuously improving your organization's awareness.*

Early in my career, I experienced attitudes toward training and development that were polar opposites. Later, as I moved into leadership positions, I gravitated toward the pole that favored developing staff and keeping them up to date on technology developments. Nonetheless, I have found that extremes rarely provide the best course, and I came to realize that an anything-goes, pro-training policy had its drawbacks.

As a young IT professional, the prevailing attitude in the companies I found myself working in was, "Training is a waste of time. You'll just get brainwashed. We need you to hustle every chance you get." At that point, having given the matter little independent thought, I pretty much agreed. I didn't think that the term "research" applied to me at all. I couldn't be bothered with a systematic investigation of the influences on the world of IT and the businesses it served.

Instead, I added to my professional knowledge in a very casual and opportunistic way. I might buy a book or get permission to go to a free presentation, but that was it. My work was my priority, and I remained connected to it even when I took a vacation.

Then I became a systems analyst at what could be considered a more progressive company. There, I learned, the CIO required every IT professional to apply for off-site training lasting at least one week each year. Any training that was at least indirectly related to your job qualified for approval, but you could also sign up for training in areas you didn't work in if it fit in with your planned future IT career direction. The CIO tied all this training to improvement of the IT organization by requiring everyone to submit a one-page report after each course taken that summarized the material and recommended changes in the IT management function that would accommodate this new knowledge.

While recognizing that the CIO was primarily interested in aggressively pursuing training because he saw it as essential in assuring continuous improvement, I was even more impressed by the psychological effect his approach had on a staff member like me. I was being trusted to manage my time so that I could accommodate the training requirement, and I was delighted that I would be paid to travel and learn. I was being given autonomy to the extent that, within limits, I could choose the material that would help me be more productive or progress my career. Best of all, I got the feeling that I would be trusted to bring back what value I could and that my input was sought. For this benefit alone, I was motivated to perform.

Over the next three years, I was trained in best practices, rapid application development techniques, database management, voice and data network integration and the latest in project management techniques. I stretched by taking a course in public speaking, something that was nerve-wracking for a typical IT introvert like me. I appreciated the wisdom of insisting that all training be done off-site, since that allowed us to concentrate without being pulled back into the comfort zone of day-to-day work.

Over time, my performance and added qualifications naturally progressed my career, and I moved up in management. And because I took pride in my growing résumé, my IT function and the enterprise I was part of, I became an enthusiastic recruiter of other IT professionals who saw the growth potential that my experience exemplified.

My colleagues and I would sometimes look back at where we had been before we had been recruited into this company and realize that we had been completely stuck; we had gone native, which is to say that we had understood that in those other companies the status quo was the priority, and change was not. More than once, co-workers would say that a former job had provided the same year of experience, again and again.

Perhaps best of all, the CIO actually implemented some of our suggestions and recognized us for bringing them to the organization's attention. This reinforced the notion that the management team was watching and actually cared about our humble proposals. And the IT function was improving its ability to perform.

By the time I moved on to leadership positions, where I could make my own decisions on things like training and development, there was no doubt in my mind that a liberal approach to training was far superior to what I had first been exposed to. I could see that it let an IT organization continuously introduce and implement beneficial change due to the staff's increased awareness. Just as important, the ground-up approach meant that change could be introduced with minimal resistance.

Nonetheless, I eventually concluded that this research and change introduction process could be improved by becoming more focused and cost-effective.

Awareness at the Root

When I moved into positions where I was responsible for others' development, I always kept in mind the idea that beneficial change (that is, improvement) is highly desirable. I also found it valuable to find out that there has been much analysis aimed at understanding how change occurs, and such analysis has always established that awareness is the first step in organizational change. In other words, there can be no change without new knowledge. And new knowledge comes to the organization through research.

One way to implement these ideas would be to follow the example of our very generous CIO, with his seemingly unlimited training budget. But normally I did not have the training budget I would need to make beneficial changes happen in the same way. And at some level, I felt that a more effective approach was possible, and even desirable.

My thinking on all of this came to fruition after I had become an application systems development manager. We knew our team had to be more productive, especially in comparison to outside firms. Faced with a limited training budget, we gathered the entire team and asked them how we could improve our productivity without the option of generous training for everyone.

What we came up with was a framework for research aimed at beneficial change. The questions we set out to research were: (a) How do we make our application development function provably the most productive on the planet?

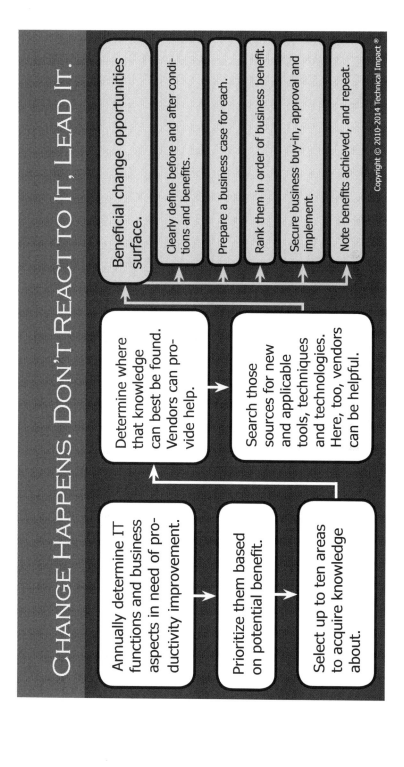

CHANGE HAPPENS. DON'T REACT TO IT, LEAD IT.

Annually determine IT functions and business aspects in need of productivity improvement.

Prioritize them based on potential benefit.

Select up to ten areas to acquire knowledge about.

Determine where that knowledge can best be found. Vendors can provide help.

Search those sources for new and applicable tools, techniques and technologies. Here, too, vendors can be helpful.

Beneficial change opportunities surface.

Clearly define before and after conditions and benefits.

Prepare a business case for each.

Rank them in order of business benefit.

Secure business buy-in, approval and implement.

Note benefits achieved, and repeat.

and (b) How do we make the businesses we serve as productive as possible?

We all agreed that to answer these questions, we would have to understand as much as possible about the latest techniques, technologies and tools, and even those still on the horizon. We also agreed that any proposed change must be practical and that we needed to prepare a short business case to clarify the return on any investment anticipated from its introduction.

Our limited training budget could then be used in a very targeted way. Instead of letting team members pursue whatever caught their interest, our training dollars went toward very specific goals. The result was much higher impact for each training dollar spent.

Of course, we could easily classify the various components of the application development process so that an environmental scan against these components would tell us how we might use our training or research dollars (or prioritize them) to gain the knowledge needed.

We were much less familiar with the needs of the business. What knowledge did we need to pursue in order to best serve it? We went in circles for a while until we realized that the best thing we could do was to ask the business itself. Those on the team most familiar with the systems that supported the business met with the business managers and came up with a list of targeted issues that they needed to address. We found that that sort of communication carries huge benefits. The business managers were enthusiastic about the new interest we were showing in their goals and processes. If anything, they felt that we should have had these sorts of discussions sooner.

With all of our planning, we were able to make the most of what we had to spend that year. We decided that ten areas were the maximum we could handle on our annual budget, leaving some things for the following year, but also putting a little money aside in case something arose unexpectedly that we needed to learn about quickly.

Our budget constraints also led us to look for ways to keep the costs of our environmental scan down, and it turned out that powerful and free knowledge-base tools were available to help us determine where the information we sought resided. Vendors were another very helpful resource, one that we had previously overlooked. Once our vendors knew what we were looking for, they were able at the very least to point us in the right general direction, again at no cost (see Chapter 6, "Just Nuke 'em," for more on getting direct access to vendor research).

Another breakthrough: We realized that we should build on the alliances we had started to create with leaders within the business by asking them to accompany us to see the new approaches we were investigating. This simple thing turned out to be a great way to shorten the time it took for the business to buy-in to the changes we proposed. As I always say, people support best what they help build. An added benefit of this approach, though, was that we could make much better matches for each business unit's particular need, and in much less time.

We understood that we would want to take a look at the landscape anew every year and decide on the areas where we would concentrate our knowledge absorption. But beyond our agreed-upon target areas, we left room for knowledge gained through individual interest, and established a process to recognize and reward anyone who improved the performance and chances for success of the IT function and the business. This turned out to be very exciting stuff for contributors, which created a desire in others to do the same.

Does It Actually Work?

Over the years, this "targeted research and change" process brought us more positive results than I could begin to tell you about. Just as an example, when I worked for a large credit card issuer, our targeted awareness and training approach led us to introduce digital imaging technology that allowed us to completely avoid the cost of handling and storing physical pieces of paper (checks) while also making it possible for call center staff to make the appropriate digital images available to customers over the Internet during a call. After the business press suggested that this was a customer service advantage, other credit card issuers hustled to duplicate and enhance the process—but we were a step ahead, and proud of it.

Yes, this improved process let us indeed measurably avoid cost, improve service, increase revenue and improve competitive advantage. What's more, its initiative was seen by the business as a proactive and practical approach to improve its value proposition to customers and help it achieve its growth strategy. Perhaps best of all, this approach to joint and purposeful exploration created positive experiences for all concerned and growing confidence that exciting discoveries were actually out there to be found. And they were.

So, here's to change. It comes to all of us, whether we expect it or not. You'll stay a step ahead of it, both for your IT function and the enterprise you serve, if you proactively and continuously improve your team's awareness. And once you've begun the process, you'll never have the same year of experience twice.

CHAPTER 24

IT Makeover: Creating an 'Attraction Strategy'

> When the CEO asks the CIO to find a way to attract the business units to the IT function, with the ultimate goal of increasing revenue, the CIO realizes his staff is going to need some new skills

The CEO who hired me as CIO to help modernize the IT function of a Fortune 500 enterprise was a visionary.

At least I thought so, and you probably would too, because he showed unusual perception about the value of IT. He didn't just want me to fix broken and outdated financial and operational support systems and to eliminate redundant IT spending that was the legacy of multiple acquisitions. He knew that bringing IT up to date was both overdue and essential to reduce IT cost, improve service, and favorably position the enterprise for additional IT-based products and services in the future.

And he hung in there even as the IT update inevitably took longer than we'd expected. But after three years, IT unit costs were down, customer service had dramatically improved, and business units were becoming interested in using IT's services a bit more to improve their productivity.

It was at that point that I saw how visionary the CEO was. Frankly, I wish I could take credit for his challenge to me. Rather than being satisfied with the improvements we had already made in the IT function, he wanted us to build on our better relations with the business units by creating an "attraction strategy." We would need to attract the business units to the IT function by demonstrating to them that we could help them improve both their business and strategic performance.

He saw IT as the best investment the enterprise could make in its quest to improve in price/performance year after year—but only if IT was focused on avoiding cost, improving service, and increasing revenue. He was able to erase any doubts in my mind with this impeccable logic: "Won't your IT unit and service cost to business units continue to decrease if the demand for your IT services continues to increase? Won't that make our overall IT asset management program more productive?"

It helped too that his last words to me at that meeting were, "Just tell me what you need."

BRM from Scratch

This all happened several years ago. Nowadays, of course, a CIO who was told to create an attraction strategy would be able to find all sorts of information about business relationship management (BRM). There is an ever-growing body of easily accessible and practical guidance about the effectiveness of a BRM function, the special talents that business relationship managers must have and keep up with, how BRMs create focus and momentum around exploiting the power of IT to improve strategic performance, and even how one can be certified as a BRM professional. Back then, though, we had to start from scratch.

But I think our experience of finding our way with so little guidance available holds valuable lessons still.

Not surprisingly, when I met with my direct reports to discuss the challenge the CEO had issued, we managed to see all kinds of snags: We weren't set up to operate like a business, we didn't have marketing or special communications resources, our staff was purpose-built around technical capabilities, we weren't deeply involved in our clients' businesses, and so on.

But a direct appeal from the CEO can't be simply shunted aside, so we kept meeting to talk about it. For a while, we just couldn't get past the difficulties that we had identified, but then someone on the team was able to turn us around by noting that knowing all of the weaknesses we were bringing to this task was actually a strength. Because we had identified them so well, we should be able to figure out what we needed to do and what resources we would require to remedy each one.

We also came to accept the following as the core principle underlying our undertaking: If the IT function was going to attract more demand, then everyone in it needed to view our business units as real customers who had a choice regarding where they obtained IT services. And if we were not directly focused on quality performance and meeting our customers' expectations, we would have no basis at all for them to seek additional IT services or assistance.

New Skills

A proposal began to take shape. We saw that we could easily scale our "plan, build and run" services to accommodate growth in demand, but it was clear that we would need significant additional resources for a new kind of client relationship management function with a different skill set than the rest of the IT function.

The new skills we were in need of were ones that could:

- Ensure that the services provided by IT remained directly responsive to the needs of every business unit it serves.
- Become active contributors to performance-improvement initiatives in the business units, and be jointly accountable for the results.
- Build a strategy to advance the priorities of both the business units and IT and thereby manage mutual expectations.
- Facilitate the provisioning of IT services, and ensure that all services remain the best means to meet business partners' needs as situations change.
- Provide all business unit staff with a directory to IT services that is always current, accessible, and readily apparent.
- Identify opportunities for the continuous improvement of IT service quality, needed adjustments to existing IT services, and all-new IT services as they become needed, and jointly assess options to arrange for and provide those services.
- Periodically give informational updates to business units regarding the advantages, features, and benefits of existing IT services and any emerging technologies, tools, or techniques that might benefit them.

In other words, if we were to create demand, we needed to add to our IT staff people who could be marketers, two-way communicators, voices of the customer, involved partners, trusted account managers, and advocates for shared services, all rolled up in one.

These new people would be the foundation of a new IT function, which we wound up calling the Business Systems Group (BSG). But the entire IT staff, bolstered by some consultative training, would play a part. Built around basic client relationship management (CRM) principles, the BSG could be the impetus, we felt, to move the IT organization toward a commercialized culture.

But how would we know if we had achieved that objective? We were aware that the CEO would want us to be able to tell him how we could be sure that our attraction strategy was working and whether or not this new BSG resource was accomplishing its mission.

What Is Success?

One part of the question of how to measure success turned out to have a simple answer, once we returned to the CEO's original request. We realized that our attraction strategy (by now we were starting to like the term) would be working if demand for our services was growing, and especially if that growth was primarily in IT's plan and build activities (in view of the CEO's emphasis on new uses of IT for improving business and strategic performance).

But measuring the BSG's success in achieving the mission we'd set for it was harder. In the end, we came up with what we considered a pretty good guess. We would quantify the BSG function's effectiveness by measuring:

- The useful knowledge it has (from a marketing viewpoint) about the business units its IT function serves.

- How the IT function is perceived by the business units it serves.
- How much the demand increases for IT services.
- The extent to which the IT function objectively introduces beneficial change throughout the business units it serves and the entire enterprise.

Expanding Our Skills

Case closed? Not really. Before approving the investment needed for the BSG (what these days we would call the BRM function), the CEO made the point that we would need to work especially hard to find the right talent and then make sure that the new skill set held by those people remained current. If we didn't, he cautioned, our new function could be seen as an additional layer of IT cost and even bureaucracy.

He was right, as usual.

As it turned out, though, over half of the BSG unit was staffed from the ranks of the existing IT team. Because those staffers needed to be proficient in interpersonal communications, they were trained in consultative skills, and the entire BSG team had to be kept up to date on critical CRM practices (all we had at the time).

Even better news was that our benchmarking processes and business unit assessments made it clear that our services were priced below the alternatives and that our approach to providing them responsively was considered anything but bureaucratic.

A Happy CEO

In the BSG's first year, demand for IT's services grew only at the same rate as before, as the BSG team became increasingly involved with the business units. At first, the BSG introduced a few small changes to business processes and built a few new (non-administrative) applications. Over the next four years, however, proportionally more IT initiatives were built to improve service and increase revenue (not just to avoid cost), and demand began to rise at a slightly higher rate. Real success came when the BSG, by virtue of its involvement with the business units, realized the power of the Internet in making our existing printed information product lines also available for sale in digital form there (I told you this was many years ago!). That initiative alone brought in significant new revenue at very little additional cost. The CEO was so pleased; the results of his IT attraction strategy became a key theme within the company's annual report to stockholders.

As the CIO, I was most pleased with the increased sense of pride among the IT team as they came to understand more directly how what they did benefited both their clients and the enterprise. And they thoroughly enjoyed the chance to be creative as part of their charge to introduce beneficial change.

NB: *To learn more about the benefits of the BRM discipline, the best places to start include: ITIL Service Management Strategy, 2011 Version (search using this term) and especially the Business Relationship Management Institute.*

Leading the Business to Better Ways

> Imagine what might happen if IT began to drive creativity and innovation.

We're already one-tenth of the way through the 21st century, so I'm sure that by now you, as an IT leader, have heard that the most productive and effective IT function is one that is directly responsive to the needs of the business it serves. You've probably heard as well that in order to best serve the business in the way it needs, the IT function must have a "client relationship management culture," not a technology culture. You might even accept the idea that IT's very existence may depend on it moving from being an isolated technology management function to being a powerful and respected ally to the business.

Nonetheless, a good many of you at this moment could be thinking, "Right. That all sounds good in theory, but it has zero application to my shop here in the real world. We're too busy responding to urgent challenges and unrelenting deadlines to think about anything like that. We just don't have the budget or the time to make it happen, and I have my doubts that the business would even understand what we were up to. Besides, what would the measures of success be? We take our direction from the business, so we'll wait for the business to tell us how to make all of that happen."

I used to think the same thing, way back in the 20th century. But then I got a wake-up call.

A Destructive Myth

It seems perfectly natural to me for IT professionals to resist the call to better understand and more fully serve the business. Like many of you, I pursued a career involving technology because I had a keen interest in it, not in business. I believed that IT professionals didn't need business acumen—a belief that's so widely held within IT's ranks that it has become a dangerous and destructive myth. Sure, I understood that the business's concern was making money, and I wanted IT to support that goal in every way it could. But anything beyond that—anything proactive rather than reactive—was not my responsibility.

My wake-up call came during a conversation with a member of the executive committee, whom I reported to. "We're very happy with how the IT function is productive and helping us avoid cost," he told me, and I was glad to hear it. But then he made it clear that the business expected more from us. "We'd be even more pleased if the IT team would occasionally bring us new ways that it could help us improve service and increase revenue." And then the kicker: "Could you see what you could do in that regard?"

Now What?

My office was in another town, and the drive gave me time to think about that message. My team and I were being asked

Building Creative Focus and Momentum

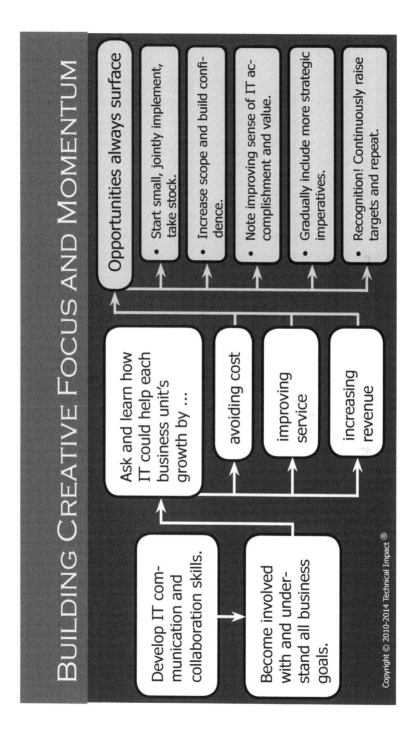

Develop IT communication and collaboration skills.
→ **Become involved with and understand all business goals.**

Ask and learn how IT could help each business unit's growth by …

- avoiding cost
- improving service
- increasing revenue

Opportunities always surface

- Start small, jointly implement, take stock.
- Increase scope and build confidence.
- Note improving sense of IT accomplishment and value.
- Gradually include more strategic imperatives.
- Recognition! Continuously raise targets and repeat.

to introduce beneficial IT changes to improve business results. We were going to be expected to take the lead, whereas until then we had always waited around for new system requirements from the business.

And I had to admit to myself that I didn't fully understand what the business's customer acquisition or retention cycles were. I had a vague notion of the business's strategy, but not to the degree that I could influence the direction of the business with IT. If my knowledge was so sketchy, I had to assume that my staff knew even less.

My team and I approached this situation in the way we were used to doing things: We treated this new directive as the latest requirement from the business, and we set about finding ways to meet it. We chose some of our application developers with the best interpersonal skills, and they set up meetings with the leaders of one strategic business unit. How, they asked them, could IT play a more effective role in their success? This seat-of-the-pants approach actually resulted in a couple of enhancements to the business unit's customer service process, and with one success behind us, we moved on to other aspects of this business unit.

It was gratifying that the business unit reported favorably on our initiative and that the executive committee heard positive things about it. But the real revelation for us was seeing the positive effect this initiative had on the IT professionals involved. They were energized by the chance to learn and be creative. They basked in newfound respect and the realization that they could have a positive impact on the business just by expanding their communication skills and by gaining business knowledge.

It was a modest beginning on the road to a proactive partnership with the enterprise, but it was irreversible, as my team's competitive spirit kicked in. And as the good word about what we were doing spread, I was able to build a compelling business case for the special expertise we needed to improve our interpersonal and consulting training skills for our too-technically-oriented IT staff. It was clear that we could not do this without experienced and proven outside transformation specialists, and we needed to ensure that our newly empowered IT professionals would be comfortable in the roles of business consultant and communicator. Though these weren't the skills our IT professionals were hired for, they were sorely needed if the IT function was to become client relationship-oriented (i.e., always ready to take the initiative, just as a partner to the business would) and have a recognized strategic business impact.

Part of IT, Proud of IT

Best of all, because all our IT professionals were being provided this transformation skills training, experienced coaching and guidance, it became obvious to them that the business actually wanted them to be fully engaged in its issues. No more destructive myth. In fact, this transformation motivated the IT professionals to perform in response, and other beneficial effects snowballed. New skills built their confidence. Ever more experience dealing in directly with business peers demonstrated their ability to contribute. Some of their ideas using emerging technologies were deemed "innovations." Once they were recognized for their initiative and achievements, their customer-oriented focus gained momentum. As results improved, their sense of accomplishment and reward improved.

Did I hear someone ask how any of this activity could be measured? As the IT function developed a client relationship management culture, we found that we could now explain all three areas of IT—plan, build and run—in terms of how they avoided cost, improved service and increased revenue. And we could demonstrate that every new initiative and contribution we undertook helped the company achieve operational excellence, customer satisfaction and positioning for industry leadership, on a continuous improvement basis.

Of course, my wake-up call came from the business, with an executive telling me what was expected from IT. But this is the 21st century, and it is now quite possible—it is even expected—that IT will take such initiatives on its own. CEOs are ever more interested in the IT function as a source of beneficial change. They have come to believe that IT can lead the business to better ways thanks to its cross-functional view of the enterprise and knowledge of emerging technologies. And they aren't likely to think much of IT managers who don't believe that themselves.

CHAPTER 26

Putting the 'B' in BRM

> *How can you have a business relationship management program that doesn't include input from the business units?*

The challenge: Justify to the senior management committee the expense of business relationship management (BRM) within the IT function.

Now, there are many ways to do that. All the tools for assessing value can be drawn upon. There's the balanced scorecard, ROI, maturity models (with key performance indicators) and assessments against them, surveys, IT investment ratios, IT productivity over time. All very plausible, given the right circumstances.

But as CIO, I knew that I had to do more than show that BRM made compelling sense from a stockholder perspective. I also had to show how its success would be measured over time.

My team and I realized that we had to be ready to answer two questions:

What strategic corporate value was there in spending

money to create a non-technical unit within IT that would be filled with people who were, all at once, IT marketers, two-way communicators, the voice of the customer, involved business-unit partners, trusted account managers, and advocates for shared IT services?

How would we know if this new IT unit's activity was successful?

Question No. 1

The best argument for the first question was that BRM would do much more than increase business-unit demand for IT services; it would also improve both business and strategic performance. We could back this up by noting that:

- Unlike nearly every other corporate expense, IT assets do more at less cost every year.
- Using IT assets effectively avoids cost, improves service and increases revenue.
- The corporation has invested significantly in IT assets, and increasing the use of those assets would improve their productivity and lower IT unit costs for the business units.
- If it is true that increasing the demand for using IT assets is beneficial, then increasing that demand should not be left to chance; however, the IT function was purpose-built around a technical skill base to supply IT services, not to create demand for those services. That requires a completely different skill set.
- Business units need to have a clear understanding of the business value of IT and be actively involved with the IT function in finding new ways to use it to improve productivity and growth.

- The primary reasons for establishing a business-oriented BRM function are to help business units understand the IT value proposition, make sure the IT function is directly responsive to business-unit needs, help business units introduce beneficial change, succeed in improving their business and strategic performance, provide a frame work for linked-destiny cooperation, collaboration, joint achievement, recognition and generate demand for effective IT services.
- It is time for the IT function to move beyond being a reactive cost center to become a proactive value adder to the business units it serves.

Question No. 2

How to know whether the BRM function was successful was a harder question to answer. It would take time for business units to go through the stages of awareness, trial, adaptation, and full acceptance of the BRM team as a true partner in helping them achieve their goals. Until we reached that final stage, measuring success wouldn't really be possible. In the end, we decided that the following would be indicators of success:

- The more knowledgeable, involved, trusted, and proactive a BRM function is, the more successful BRM is.
- The more BRM helps IT's clients improve their business and strategic performance, the more successful BRM is.
- The more demand increases for the strategic use of IT assets, the more successful BRM is.

One More Question

We had done our homework well enough to get the funding we wanted from the senior management committee to establish the BRM role if we could answer just one more question: "What are the risks associated with implementing this BRM role in corporate IT, and how would we deal with each of those risks?"

That wasn't the SMC telling us to go back to the drawing board. In fact, it was exactly the right question to ensure eventual success. The SMC was letting us know that they understood and supported our proposal and wanted it to succeed. To that end, my team and the committee would be jointly reviewing how we were going to address the implementation challenges ahead.

Executive Sponsorship Is Not Enough

Energized by the SMC's request, my team took our initial BRM implementation plan and added much more detail. We dug deep and found several previously uncontemplated situations we might run into, and we described how we would address each of them. Far more importantly, it soon became blindingly clear that we hadn't fully addressed what was needed to obtain long-lasting buy-in from our business-unit clients (soon to be partners, we hoped), nor had we budgeted enough time to properly secure it.

This was a problem, we realized; certainly it was essential to have the blessing of the SMC and executive sponsorship for the BRM initiative, but without buy-in from the business units, it would never amount to a thing. We would have to slow things down, but clearly we had a compelling reason to do so. We had to carefully identify and plan for what it would take to obtain from the business units their understanding, support, involvement, and joint accountability (ownership) of the BRM program. This was a bump in our road, but we felt no inclination to curse it. To the contrary, we were very thankful for the SMC's directive to consider our risks carefully. Without that guidance, we might have barreled ahead without properly addressing what was probably our most important critical success factor.

People Support Best What They Help Build

We knew now that we had to involve and pull the business units into our implementation plan. We had to explain the BRM capability and ensure all had a common understanding of its future benefits as compared to our current state. We had to show how it would affect interactions between the business units and IT. We had to demonstrate its business value. Each business unit would be invited to join us in sessions to work on the implementation plan, walk through those plans as they were developed, and provide feedback as we progressed. We also added a formal milestone in the schedule where each business unit would be allowed to approve or suggest changes to the BRM mission (outlined in the sidebar).

After reviewing everything we could think of several times, we scheduled our next SMC session.

What Happened?

The SMC was pleased. They helpfully pointed out some things in our plan that could use some attention, and they offered their help if needed, but our BRM implementation was on its way. One SMC member termed the additional time we'd added for our business-unit collaboration sessions, as "essential missionary work."

And so it proved. The time we'd added for involving, sharing, understanding and addressing questions from the busi-

Proposed BRM Mission

The BRM team will:

• Ensure that the services provided by IT remain directly responsive to the needs of every business unit it serves.

• Become active contributors to performance-improvement initiatives in the business units, and be jointly accountable for the results.

• Build a strategy to advance the priorities of both the business units and IT and thereby manage mutual expectations.

• Facilitate the provisioning of IT services, and ensure that all services remain the best means to meet business partners' needs as situations change.

• Provide all business-unit staff with a directory to IT services that is always current, accessible and readily apparent.

• Identify opportunities for the continuous improvement of IT service quality, needed adjustments to existing IT services, and all-new IT services as they become needed, and jointly assess options to arrange for and provide those services.

• Periodically give informational updates to business units regarding the advantages, features, and benefits of existing IT services and any emerging technologies, tools, or techniques that might benefit them.

ness units and exchanging concerns with them enabled us to adjust things (even in small ways) so that we were more in harmony with each business unit's particular IT and business situations.

Shortly, business-unit staffers were applying for positions within the BRM team. That was when we knew that accountability for the success of the BRM program was becoming shared with our new business partners.

And it was a pleasant surprise to find how all this led to ever more cooperation between the IT function and the business units, as we began to work as a unified team to address business challenges together. The business units got comfortable with using the IT assets and resources available to them and, just as important, the IT folks started to want to prove the value of their function in this new role.

CHAPTER 27

To Whom Should the CIO Report?

> Imagine if the strategic engine of the enterprise didn't report to the CEO.

The question has been batted back and forth for nearly as long as there have been CIOs: To whom should they report? I won't keep you in suspense as to where I stand: CIOs hold a C-level position, and as such they should report to the strategic leader, meaning either the CEO or the COO.

Why do I believe this? I have several reasons, and none of them has anything to do with status. The simplest is this: Because information technology is the most powerful competitive enabler available to most businesses, its leader should not be relegated to reporting to someone who may have other priorities than the organization's strategic performance.

There are some exceptions to this, and I'll get to them. But first, let me articulate the primary reasons why having the CIO report directly to the CEO is the best arrangement.

1. CFOs have totally different priorities.

CFOs are, by nature, risk-averse. They are charged with protecting the financial well-being of the organization. Their charter is to question expenditures, ensure that proper controls are in place and ascertain that investments realize the expected returns. Their focus is on the short term, and their priority is process. CIOs, on the other hand, *must* be risk takers. After all, every strategic system development project is risky—it has never been done before in the company and will have long-term impact. CIOs have to focus on the long term, since most significant IT developments span many years. Their priority is introducing beneficial change, not maintaining a consistent process. When a CIO reports to the CFO, the IT function ends up operating much more conservatively than it should. That might be okay for certain companies, on a temporary basis, and in the course of my career as a CIO, I had some productive working relationships with CFOs that I reported to. Nonetheless, I think that the days when this sort of relationship could really work are gone. Quite frankly, a conservative IT function is not going to help most companies to confront the increasingly intense competitive environment out there.

2. The CEO needs to know what IT can do for the company.
Strategic IT projects can have an enormous impact on the future of a company. That makes the IT function so central to the company's competitiveness that it's essential for the CEO to have a working knowledge of the process of IT project creation. This is too important to be blunted by intermediaries. A CEO needs a CIO who can function as a partner, giving the CEO enough familiarity with the process of IT project creation so that the CEO can make sure that the company's strategy is being properly addressed by the IT function.

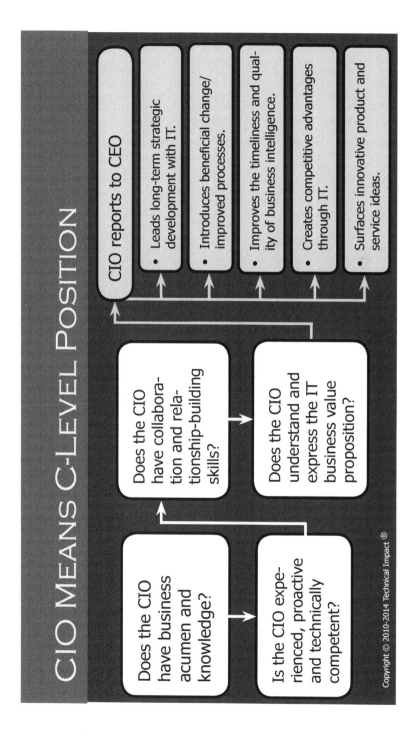

3. CIOs need to be deeply involved in business operations.

The officers who are closest to the operations side of the business are the CEO and COO. Most CEOs today want their CIO to help the business compete profitably through technology, and they recognize that the CIO can better do this when enmeshed in the inner operations of the lines of business. A CIO reporting to the CFO or CAO misses out on working closely with people who are savvy about those things.

4. CIOs need credence in the eyes of users.

Most internal IT customers are part of the operational staff. A CIO who is positioned on the same side of the org chart as them has more credence.

5. Reporting to the CEO provides enterprise-wide purview.

Because IT is the strategic engine of the business, its priorities must be set with the participation of all parts of the organization. When the CIO reports to the CEO, the other C-level executives understand that relationship.

6. Reporting to the CEO gives the CIO more influence.

Influence should not be confused with status. Status resides inside people's heads, but influence has real practical value. A CIO might need to make significant organizational changes, possibly even cultural changes. Anything that affects the status quo is likely to meet major resistance, and a CIO who is working hand in hand with the CEO is better able to carry out initiatives effectively. When everyone knows that the CIO reports to the CEO, they perceive that the CEO accords the IT function and the CIO position a great deal of importance. And when any part of the business has a problem with what IT is doing, the CIO can set up a meeting with the CEO quickly.

7. No one but the CEO is going to adequately support the research the CEO wants the CIO to deliver.
Increasingly, CEOs want their CIOs to help lead the business to better ways of doing things through new ideas and technologies. But it's unlikely that any other C-level officer is going to fully recognize how vitally important researching emerging technologies is, and they certainly would be slow to come up with the necessary funding.

When Is a CIO Not a CIO?
Case closed? Actually, no. There are instances when a CIO shouldn't be in a close relationship with the CEO and should instead report to someone else. What this comes down to is the qualifications of the CIO, plus the CEO's definition of a C-level position. In other words, there are CIOs who hold the title but aren't really considered to function at the C level.

A C-level CIO is not just technically competent. Such CIOs are also proactive in their technical competence, display business leadership abilities and are skilled in collaboration, communication and persuasion. They know how to create relationships out of a community of interest in profitably growing the business, and they are able to jump-start initiatives to move the business to higher competitive levels. In other words, they have considerable business acumen and are able to talk about their specialty in the business and stockholder terms that their peers understand.

CIOs who lack these skills—who cannot clearly articulate how the IT function benefits business results by avoiding cost, improving service and increasing revenue—should report to an executive other the CEO. CIOs just don't belong on that level of management if they are unable to convert strategic and business direction into IT actions. These CIOs are really technology-focused IT managers who do not understand all aspects of the business value proposition. They cannot be expected to fully develop the initiatives the organization needs to derive from its IT function, and frankly, I've found that such technology-focused IT managers will not take such initiatives in any case.

The trend today seems to be toward more and more CIOs who truly belong on the C level, with some of them holding broad general business management positions. Some examples: The CIO of one of the largest IT equipment suppliers also directs his firm's supply chain; the CIO for a major airline is responsible for all marketing activities; the CIO for a major parcel-delivery company is also responsible for route acquisition and optimization.

What they all have in common, besides a deep understanding of the business and how to communicate in business terms, is that they all report to their CEO.

CHAPTER 28

IT Gets Its Report Card

> *The IT leader who can't explain where the IT function is and where it should be won't be around for long.*

IT leaders at all levels, right up to the CIO, need to be prepared to respond to their toughest critics. That may be the CEO, another C-level officer or even the company chairman. One of these people, one of these days, is going to confront you with some very to-the-point questions about what IT is doing, what it should be doing, and how the IT function can perform for the business better. It would be wise to think about those questions now, so that, when the time comes, you will be ready with answers that demonstrate that this is not the first time you have contemplated such questions.

The toughest question of all, the one whose multiple parts get to the heart of how you should be thinking about the IT function, goes something like this: "Is our IT function where it needs to be? Do we even know where it needs to be? And how will we know when we get there?"

Your answer to this big question cannot be equivocal, and

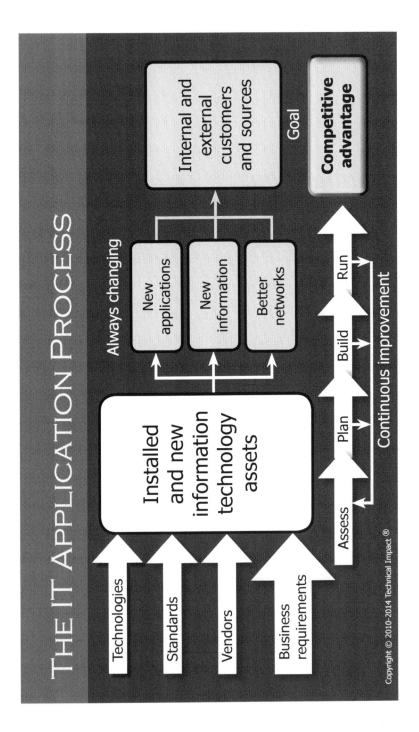

THE IT APPLICATION PROCESS

Technologies

Standards

Vendors

Business requirements

Installed and new information technology assets

Always changing

New applications

New information

Better networks

Internal and external customers and sources

Goal

Competitive advantage

Assess — Plan — Build — Run

Continuous improvement

Copyright © 2010-2014 Technical Impact ®

for your response to be both satisfactory *and* useful in the future, it must be delivered in the language of business.

At the very least, you need to be able to say that the IT function is actively striving to be where it needs to be, but because the business it serves is itself always evolving, the IT function must constantly be reassessed. The important things are to understand the direction it should be moving in, and to realize that improvement must be constant.

We know the IT function is moving in the right direction when:

- Business leaders perceive it as a powerful ally to the enterprise.
- It is seen to be continually helping the enterprise avoid cost, improve service and increase revenue.
- We are certain that each IT investment we make will improve the enterprise's value proposition to its customers, employees and stockholders.

Those are goals, but how do we reach them? The answer is by always being a highly effective IT function. But that just raises yet another question, namely, how do we define a highly effective IT function? To my mind, this is a matter of attitude, direction and structure. These three things are all vitally important, and it's crucial to understand the part that each plays in making IT effective. Ignore one, and IT will be out of balance. Achieving the right combination is imperative. An IT function with a perfect structure and a great attitude can still go off the rails if it's taking the wrong direction.

You can think of these three aspects as categories on a report card. The higher the grade that IT receives in each of them, the more directly connected and responsive the IT function will be to business needs. And an "F" in any one of

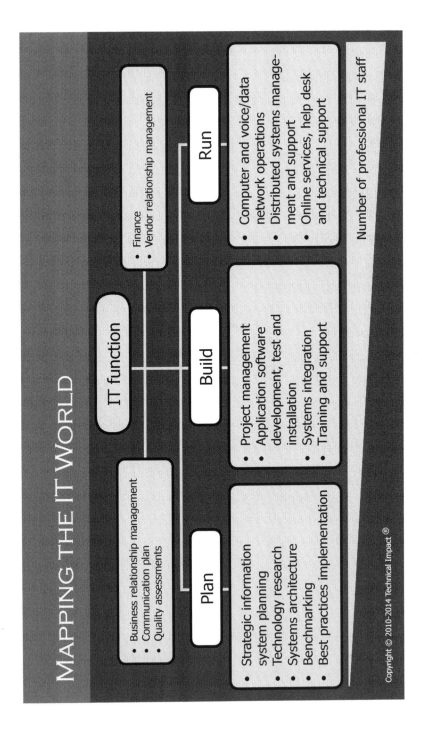

MAPPING THE IT WORLD

IT function

Plan
- Strategic information system planning
- Technology research
- Systems architecture
- Benchmarking
- Best practices implementation

Build
- Project management
- Application software development, test and installation
- Systems integration
- Training and support

- Business relationship management
- Communication plan
- Quality assessments

- Finance
- Vendor relationship management

Run
- Computer and voice/data network operations
- Distributed systems management and support
- Online services, help desk and technical support

Number of professional IT staff

them means IT could be held back, and is probably holding the business back.

The most concrete of these three aspects of IT is structure, so let's begin there.

Show Me the Structure

The chart on the opposite page, with its three branches of "Plan," "Build" and "Run," illustrates the basic structure of a well-organized IT function.

As those three branches suggest, the IT function is organized by responsibilities. Assuming you have sufficient head count, you want to have a group that plans the systems the business needs, another that builds those systems, and a third to run the systems once they have been implemented. I didn't invent this organizational scheme; it's been addressed in countless books. But I've found it to be a highly effective way to meet the needs of the enterprise.

The chart also shows that various IT functions are grouped within the plan, build and run domains. In practice, with the right direction and attitude, the details of this compartmentalization will eventually arrange themselves optimally. Nonetheless, it's good to start with such groupings, as useful checklists.

And remember, even if you devise the perfect structure, it will mean nothing by itself. Without the proper attitude and direction, an IT function can become a bureaucratic nightmare, actually stifling the growth of the business and using up considerable time and financial resources.

You don't want that.

Attitude Adjustment

Of the three aspects of the IT function, attitude may be the most important. The attitude you want to foster is one where the customer, and not technology, is the focus. The professionals within the IT function should feel that IT has no destiny separate from the business units it serves. They will declare IT a success only when the business units it serves are successful.

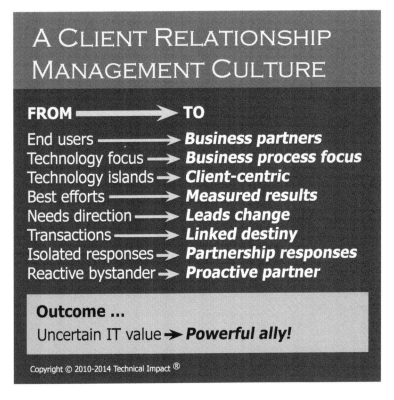

A CLIENT RELATIONSHIP MANAGEMENT CULTURE

FROM ➡ TO	
End users ➡	*Business partners*
Technology focus ➡	*Business process focus*
Technology islands ➡	*Client-centric*
Best efforts ➡	*Measured results*
Needs direction ➡	*Leads change*
Transactions ➡	*Linked destiny*
Isolated responses ➡	*Partnership responses*
Reactive bystander ➡	*Proactive partner*

Outcome ...
Uncertain IT value ➡ *Powerful ally!*

Copyright © 2010-2014 Technical Impact ®

Attitudes are reflected in language. Take a look at the chart above. You know your IT function is where you want it to be when the terms used in discussions by and about IT move from those on the left side of the chart to those on the right side.

Please know that some training in business communication and something called "best practices" are short cuts to

TARGETING YOUR IT MANAGEMENT FACTORS

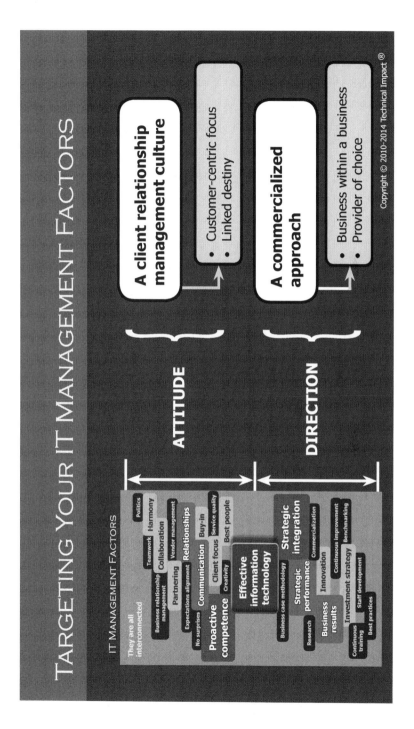

IT MANAGEMENT FACTORS

A client relationship management culture

- Customer-centric focus
- Linked destiny

ATTITUDE

A commercialized approach

- Business within a business
- Provider of choice

DIRECTION

the outcomes on the right (See Chapter 14).

The more you hear the terms on the right, the higher the grades given to the IT function's attitude.

How do you instill this attitude? Leading by example is important, but so is a constant focus on business-IT "win-win" collaboration activities and the adoption and continued use of best practices. But be assured, once this transformation begins in earnest, it is irreversible, and ever more beneficial IT initiatives will surface from the IT function over time.

Asking for Directions

With the right structure and attitude, you might think nothing can go wrong. But it can if you haven't assured that the IT function is moving in the right direction.

Imagine an IT function that is conducted as a business, not with captive clients or even virtual clients, but with clients who can choose between using the corporate IT function or something else.

Such an IT function would unambiguously understand that the direction it needs to follow is to be a commercialized entity, earning a reputation as the IT service provider of choice. Perhaps the business unit leaders in your enterprise don't have such a stark choice between your IT function and something else, but all IT functions should be oriented toward being a commercialized entity. They need to always be considered as a commercial business partner that is creative and proactive about driving out cost and continually improving responsiveness.

It might sound like a difficult task to help IT professionals develop business acumen. Good news: It isn't. In fact, time and again I have witnessed IT professionals rise to this challenge. They actually *want* to know more about how they can aid the business they work for, at every level.

Try it and see for yourself. Once you have directed the IT function to commercialize itself, things will happen quickly. Your staff will establish lines of service business. They will figure out what's important to IT's clients. They will set up the structure and capacity to provide it. And they will calculate the costs associated with providing it.

You'll also want the IT function to start to benchmark itself against commercial alternatives to determine whether it has the advantage in costs for services and, if that advantage is lacking, to understand why it doesn't measure up.

As a commercialized entity, the IT function will naturally develop new priorities, such as focusing on cost control. You will find that no projects are proposed if they would incur an IT cost that does not have a clear and direct relationship to successful customer outcomes.

You will know for sure that the IT function is moving in the right direction when the staff raises the idea of offering senior management a kind of annual report on IT performance that uses terms such as *operational excellence, client satisfaction, positioning for the future* and *industry leadership.*

And your IT function will deserve a high grade on its report card. (For more on the IT commercialization framework and how to begin and continue this transformation process, see Chapter 18, "There's No Lasting Change Without Buy-In," page 137.)

Getting There

Clearly, a proactive IT leader will be on top of all these issues before ever getting those tough questions about where the IT function ought to be. It's likely, in fact, that a proactive IT leader will preclude the need for anyone to ask those questions by bringing up the topic himself. The important thing, though, is to anticipate the need to address such issues and to

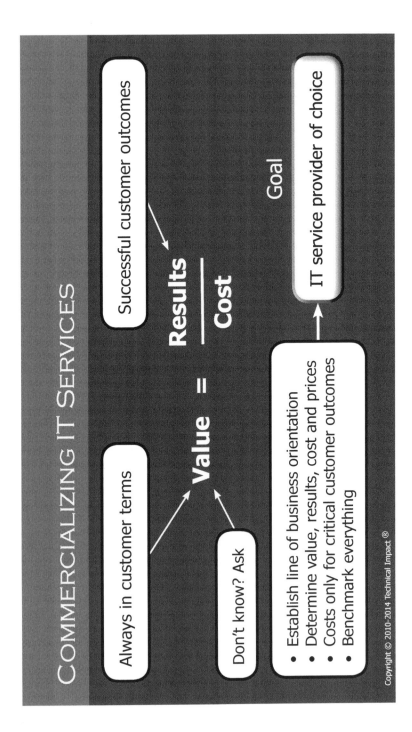

COMMERCIALIZING IT SERVICES

Successful customer outcomes

Always in customer terms

$$Value = \frac{Results}{Cost}$$

Don't know? Ask

Goal

IT service provider of choice

- Establish line of business orientation
- Determine value, results, cost and prices
- Costs only for critical customer outcomes
- Benchmark everything

recognize that the answer must be to make the IT function a full and responsive part of the business that has a responsibility to help it achieve its goals.

I'm an advocate of the proactive approach, of course, and in my view, getting the answers to these questions out to the business-unit executives is IT marketing in action. You want to keep these questions from being asked by eliminating the need to ask them—everyone will already know the answers.

The same goes for that ultimate shareholder question: "Can an outside IT service firm do what our IT function does cheaper or faster or better?" And if you're getting good grades (and steadily improving) on your IT report card, then your IT function has some profound strategic advantages to the enterprise over most for-hire IT firms.

These advantages need to be understood by all IT function staff (and just as they will want to develop their business acumen, they will enjoy knowing about how to sell the IT function), and they need to communicate them periodically with all levels of their client community. In other words, they need to market the IT function.

What makes a high-performing IT function really different from an outside IT service provider? It's a mix of several things, including the following:

- **The IT function has extensive resources and staying power.**

I've found it an extremely useful exercise to direct the IT team to draw up an inventory of the IT function's proven capabilities and performance. When your team does this themselves, they internalize this information, and the opportunities to share it with others in the enterprise are endless. This exercise also has an effect on the IT team's pride.

Make sure the team doesn't over look the IT function's

stability in their inventory. IT service firms come and go. They get acquired, or they end with so many clients that they can't give you the proper attention. In other words, a high-performing internal IT function can be relied upon to be the safe and dependable choice for all enterprise needs.

- **It offers services not found elsewhere.**

Here's another inventory that will open eyes. Every internal IT function that I have been familiar with has done things for strategic business units that no outside IT service provider will do—and some things that you might be able to get an outside firm to do, but only at great cost, after a custom bidding process.

- **It is free of vendor bias.**

An internal IT function will choose the best price/performance vendor for the enterprise's needs, no matter what. Have you ever known an IT systems integration or facilities management service that didn't recommend its parent company's IT products?

- **It has one priority: Internal enterprise clients.**

An IT function has no other clients to keep happy. You won't be subjected to any trade-offs that might arise because of potentially conflicting service levels. And an internal IT function has no financial secrets, making it easy for business units and the enterprise as a whole to manage their cost structure.

- **It is committed to quality and continuous improvement.**

A high-performing internal IT function will establish yearly targets for continuously improving productivity and client satisfaction, and it will objectively show progress. Will you routinely see this kind of initiative from outside IT contract service firms? No.

- **It has a business orientation and knows its clients' needs.**

Because a high-performing IT function is commercialized and run like a business, its clients' business needs are readily apparent to the IT team. The team knows the enterprise's client acquisition cycle, its retention process, its strategic performance goals and all the rest.

- **It is easy to buy from.**

Whenever a business unit has to contract with an outside service provider, settling accounts is complicated. Expenses have to be tracked and monitored. Discrepancies eat up time and other resources. Reconciling items on an invoice can be burdensome. And you don't even want to think about what happens anytime Legal has to get involved.

- **Because it doesn't seek profit, it is the lowest-cost alternative.**

Benchmarking, done properly, compares the cost of specific internal IT functions to the cost of those same services performed by outside firms. Because any outside IT service firm will necessarily require a high gross profit margin, external IT costs will normally be higher, sometimes significantly so. In the rare cases when a specific internal IT service cost is not lower, the high-performing IT function will find out why and either fix the problem immediately it or use the lower-cost outside service until it can fix it.

As with all marketing efforts, the core message of IT performance marketing will need to be updated and repeated. But I can assure you that as you effectively deliver your message, your audience will be looking forward to knowing more about your high-performing IT function.

Obviously, much more could be said about all of this, and it's more complicated than I've led you to believe. There is a lot that I could tell you about how to take IT effectiveness measurement to even higher levels (including targeted quality, efficiency and productivity measures). But you don't have to be a rocket scientist to know that the sooner the IT function understands its mission in such terms, can articulate its true value proposition to the business and becomes a powerful ally in achieving business goals, the better for everyone, including the stockholder.

Will being part of such a transforming achievement have an effect on anyone's résumé?

Yes, but only in positive ways.

Career Craft

> To keep your IT career moving forward and challenging, you must never stop learning—what got you to your current position won't get you to the next one.

I wasn't born a CIO, of course. There are many routes to that position, but in my case the stops along the way included computer operator, computer operations supervisor, programmer, systems programmer, systems analyst, applications development team leader, project manager, director of network and computer operations, and director of management information systems. And CIO wasn't the end of the story, either, since I followed that with being a business manager and a consultant.

I should also say that I haven't written this book as a blueprint for becoming a CIO. I don't actually believe that there can be such a thing. Nor do I believe that everyone in IT wants to be a CIO, or that that is the only way to effect change and achieve satisfaction in a career in IT. What I do believe is that there are proven ways to make IT effective in serving the business, thus making IT an active and appreciated partner in the business. But I didn't wake up one day to suddenly find myself in possession of all of the knowledge necessary to do that. I built it up gradually, sometimes painfully slowly, but always consciously, because I was (and am to this day) dedicated to a lifetime of constant learning and reevaluation.

More than any specific lessons, the message I hope this book delivers is that the key to success for IT professionals who want to move their careers along is to always be willing, able and hungry to learn.

What I was learning changed as I went along. In my early days, I was mostly caught up in learning about the job at hand, but as an ambitious and curious sort, also learning about this organism that was the IT organization. My impetus then was to discover how I could best position myself to move up to the positions I coveted, with not a thought toward IT's role in the overall business, but in that process I was laying the groundwork for all that came later. My education about what could be called the bigger picture began in earnest when I took my first big leap, reaching out for what seemed like an exciting adventure that turned into that and more.

The adventure began in what I thought of as a pretty fancy waiting room. My own workspace was a small cubicle sitting alongside many other cubicles. I was, by others' assessment, a pretty good systems programmer who had recently been promoted. But I was looking for a change, and I thought that this prestigious IT systems integration firm whose waiting room I was now sitting in might have a job for me or a contract that I might fit into. I had gathered up my courage and set up a "blind date" interview.

While I was admiring my surroundings, a nice gentleman, whose name was Ollie, came along and introduced himself.

Was I interviewing for the new major IT project in Hawaii? he wanted to know.

It wasn't the question I had expected, but my body language must have indicated that I was certainly interested, because Ollie took me by the arm and led me into the office of the Hawaii project's hiring manager. His name was Irwin, and he told me that the Hawaii project needed skilled computer programmers to fix big-time systems that hadn't been built properly. As a systems programmer, I was overqualified, but the prospect of living outside of California for the first time in my life, in Hawaii of all places, was simply too enticing. I agreed on the spot, only pondering as I headed home what my wife, who had never even been on a plane, would think of this disruption to our lives.

Disruption? Well, my life was definitely never the same after that. Never again would I spend quiet, risk-free days as a generally isolated technician. I was able to help the big systems integration company perform on this contract, which led to ever more responsibility, assignments and reward. Eventually, my career would take us to great American cities like New York, Los Angeles and Chicago, to world capitals like Washington, Ottawa, Brussels, London and Paris, and to places of great natural beauty like Florida and Hawaii.

In the end, did it matter that I was once a computer operator or programmer earlier in my career? Did it matter that I was not only qualified but a little more so to get on the plane to go to Hawaii for a few years? Did it matter that every single assignment I ever had built on what I'd learned previously, even though this previous learning was stressful at times? Did it matter that when I became a manager I knew what it was like to be an IT professional at every level and what it felt like to be in their shoes?

Oh, yes, it mattered. The things I had learned in every position mattered a lot, and on several levels. Allow me to give you a short review of the course of my career.

Mapping the IT World

In Chapter 17 of this book, I talk about targeting a position of strategic consequence. But you aren't going to land a position of strategic consequence until you yourself are a person of consequence. You need a background that tells potential employers that they won't be wasting their time listening to your side of the employment equation.

As I indicated above, my background was broad. I often use the terms "plan, build and run" to segment the management of the major IT functions, but they are also a useful framework when you are considering IT career options and opportunities (see chart "Mapping the IT World," page 196).

I have spent parts of my professional life in each of these three IT domains, so I know that the critical success factors for each are very different, meaning that they require different skills and attract people of different dispositions. If you are trying to establish yourself and move your career along with care, it is helpful to understand these differences.

Certainly, people involved in planning and building IT (developing it) have a fundamentally different mind-set and skills than those who run IT (operate it daily).

The best people to run IT (computer, telecommunications, network, computer distributed system operations) are those who are, by disposition, very sensitive to the ever-changing operational situation around them. They know that they cannot afford to be overly reflective about a burgeoning problem, and they are very comfortable with taking decisions early. They struggle valiantly to maintain IT services at a high performance level, work that is often complicated by the need to supply round-the-clock services to a 24/7/365 enterprise that operates in multiple time zones. They are on the job very early to accommodate a review of the previous shift's log so that they know about any legacy problems or things to watch and to get a good hand-off from the management of the previous shift. They attend meetings before each shift to both formalize the hand-off process and to do a kind of postmortem on things that need a root-cause analysis. When they know that key operations staff won't be available, they call in alternatives in advance, sometimes three levels deep. IT "run" professionals are tuned in to transaction volume, network availability and response time on a moment-by-moment basis. They are focused on avoiding critical situations before they develop, making sure that there is no single point of failure, that they are never out of capacity, that they always have backup.

That might sound hectic, but run functions are anything but seat-of-the-pants operations. In fact, thanks to the look-ahead tools that are now available to ensure IT operations reliability, IT run functions normally have a deliberate, professional and almost serene quality about them.

The other thing about run operations is that they are a good place to earn your initial reputation.

As for IT planning and building, they require a much more reflective disposition and a very different skill set. Time sensitivity remains essential, but it has a different character when you are measuring project progress on a weekly and monthly basis. People in the plan and build functions need interpersonal skills because they are called upon to translate business issues (requirements) into automated solutions. Throughout the development process, they must meet with their business clients to make sure that the resulting automated solution (called an application) does what it's supposed to when it is completed and operational. The mantra of the IT plan and build functions is: applications software delivered on time, as specified and for the agreed cost. To these IT professionals, knowledge of the IT "run" world is useful, but not essential. However, knowledge of project management and the latest and most productive application software development techniques and tools is mandatory.

Sounds calm and complacent, doesn't it? Well, it is for a while, and then it's not. If you want to see a bit of hectic activity, watch an applications software development team, with the operational deadline looming, go through that phase of their effort called operational readiness testing.

Plotting a Course

At the dawn of my career, I knew that I loved being around IT and helping people who seemed a bit afraid of it understand its power. I decided that I liked the application development side of the IT world, and I committed myself to find my profession there.

Not a chance. Entry-level positions surfaced from time to time, but I had no practical experience. I had learned how to program applications software from training manuals. Hiring managers did not find that to be a compelling reason to make me their next developer.

Contemplating my dilemma, I did a little research into the structure of IT itself, and I started to learn about the plan, build and run functions, as described above. I could see that the IT plan function employed the fewest IT professionals (i.e., strategic IT planners, client relationship managers, service quality specialists), and other than management, they were the highest paid. But their qualifications were towering in terms of practical previous experience. There was no such thing as an entry-level job in the plan arena.

The next largest group in any IT organization usually

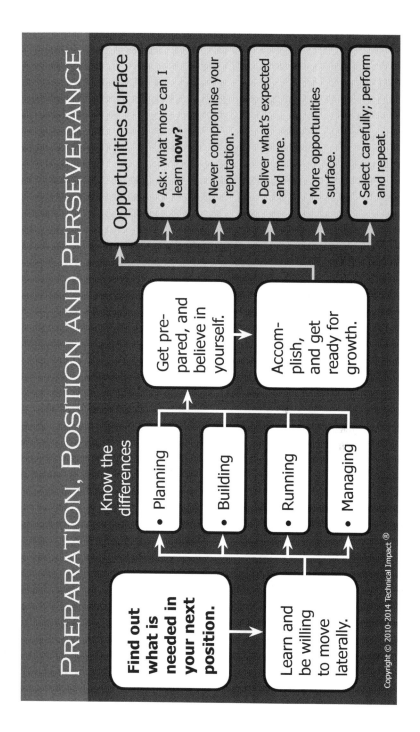

PREPARATION, POSITION AND PERSEVERANCE

Find out what is needed in your next position.

Learn and be willing to move laterally.

Know the differences

- Planning
- Building
- Running
- Managing

Get prepared, and believe in yourself.

Accomplish, and get ready for growth.

Opportunities surface

- Ask: what more can I learn **now?**
- Never compromise your reputation.
- Deliver what's expected and more.
- More opportunities surface.
- Select carefully; perform and repeat.

worked in the IT build function. These folks (i.e., programmers, analysts, project managers, system architects) were also very well paid, and their qualifications were also high. An entry-level job wasn't impossible in the build arena, but I would need a lot of luck. Even though build was my preferred IT area, I didn't like the odds at all.

By far, the largest number of IT professionals in any IT function was in the IT run area. But they were paid less than in the other functions, though the qualifications required were lower as well, and entry-level positions were out there. I became a computer operator in short order, and because the company offered training and tuition reimbursement, I learned more about the IT applications development "build" skills in a gradual way. Best of all, I found out that most IT build functions preferred to go to their own IT run functions when they needed people with a demonstrated good performance profile for their entry-level openings!

And so, by learning a bit about how things worked, I set my course, and once I got in the field, I never stopped learning. That, more than anything, is what kept me moving along to ever more challenges. In fact, the question, "What am I going to learn?" is probably a good one to ask yourself as you consider each new opportunity before you.

And believe me, there is plenty of learning to be done. Along my way, I learned why it was important to jump at the chance to work for and with the people who embrace learning as much as you do and who are excited about the work they're doing (see Chapter 12, "Of Operators and Performers"). I found out how to best communicate the power of IT's contribution in simple and positive business terms (see Chapter 2, "What Are You Doing for Me, and Why Don't I Know It?" and Chapter 7, "Tell Your Story Plain to Win Over the Business Managers").

I figured out the key factors that enable an enthusiastic, creative and empowered team, and how to keep it that way (see Chapter 15, "Leading by Letting Go"). I learned why it was essential to take the initiative in building relationships with business managers (see Chapter 3, "Reactive Bystander, or Proactive Partner?"). I discovered practical ways to transform the IT function so that it performed as a business-within-a-business, as well as how to constructively start this transformation process (see Chapter 18, "There's No Lasting Change Without Buy-in").

I went to school on best practices, quality and continuous improvement, learning how to make the IT function ever more effective for the business by getting IT professionals to feel "part of it, proud of it" (see Chapter 14, "Getting the Best Out of IT Best Practices" and Chapter 21 "The Case for Quality'). I got an education on how to develop a genuine spirit of collaboration between corporate and strategic business units and so improve IT's effectiveness and productivity (see Chapter 13, "Can We Please Get Everyone to Speak the Same Language?"). And I learned that actively seeking beneficial change by exploring emerging tools, techniques and technologies is both enjoyable and extremely good for business (see Chapter 23, "Directing Discovery").

I learned all of that, and much, much more. Something every day, I'd say.

Albert Einstein said, "I never teach my pupils; I only attempt to provide the conditions in which they can learn." I won't presume to teach you. Instead, I hope I have helped you recognize the conditions that will facilitate learning throughout your IT career. If you foster those conditions, you will continuously enhance your ability to contribute at ever higher levels. Just be prepared as well to deal with an ever increasing number of opportunities.

CHAPTER 30

Get the IT Career You Want by Developing Your Business Value

If you're working in IT today, technical proficiency will never be enough.

Alot of technology professionals are frustrated with the IT profession. They can't find a job or move into the position that they want. They're always hearing that demand exists, but that's not what their personal experience has shown them. They feel they have the skills for the job, and have even put in the time it takes to be qualified or certified in the technologies in demand. But the requirements for IT career development remain elusive.

For some IT professionals, the frustration has mounted to the point that they are at a loss as to what they need to do to fit into the future of a profession they have devoted themselves to. Abandon the IT profession? I don't think so. In today's economic conditions, with ever more intense competition and the ever-faster emergence of new technologies, the demand for people who can effectively apply IT to business needs and strategic goals has never been greater.

But notice that I didn't say that business simply needs IT practitioners. It does, but more specifically, it requires "people who can effectively apply IT to business needs and strategic goals." The IT professionals that employers consider to be valuable to their business have not only the right technical skills, but also the capabilities needed for *productive business contributions over the long term.*

But what about those seemingly mysterious criteria for the jobs you want? It's straightforward really. You need to demonstrate that you are aware of business needs and can find new and innovative ways to achieve them. You need to speak the language of business. And just as you have always fortified yourself with training in the latest technologies, you need to consistently apply yourself to the acquisition of the softer skills needed to:

- Communicate in business terms;
- Be a better leader in the enterprise;
- Negotiate the client ecosystem efficiently;
- Inspire your team; and
- Become invaluable to the success of your clients.

Are you not happy to have so much more to learn? Well, the good news about the soft skills that are critical to the development of IT careers is that, unlike technology skills, they do not change. In fact they continue to build on themselves. And if you've been ignoring them in favor of more and more hard-skill certifications, then you have been limiting yourself in the marketplace, because these career-building skills are increasingly considered *more valuable* to employers than technical proficiency. In other words, you need both, and if all you have is technical proficiency—even extraordinary technical proficiency—you are going nowhere. But if you pair that technical proficiency with extraordinary business awareness and responsiveness, then the sky is the limit.

Know Where You Want to Go

Early on in my own career, I relied on what I call the "lucky shotgun" approach to career choices. I would pursue various training opportunities that appealed to me or seemed promising, and I pursued every opportunity for advancement that came along. For a time, it worked very well, and I felt that I was being carried along by forward momentum despite any real plan. Eventually, though, my progress slowed and I started second-guessing my career decisions. That's when someone told me that I should know what I was looking for before I started looking. I've since heard this expressed memorably as "If you don't know your destination, any road will do."

Taking that advice to heart, I started to develop conscious intent, which allowed me to make steady small steps with the potential to make me a more attractive option when an opportunity that fit with my goals arose. I developed a series of short-term, highly specific goals that I could prepare myself for, and the achievement of each one made me feel once again that I was on the move. Of course, at the same time I held on to a more vague long-term goal, but achieving it instantly was not my focus. You could think of all this as akin to being on a riverbank. You want to work your way upstream, and you have a general idea that you might want to be on the other side of the river at some point. But standing on your riverbank, you can only see as far as the next bend, and that's your immediate goal. Eventually, after reaching many bends, you might work your way to a place where you can easily get across the river. Try it too soon, though, and you just might end up in a backwater—or even washed back downstream.

Defining Goals

So, be specific, and be realistic. You have to set achievable objectives, so that you establish a pattern of success.

Consider everything, and when you decide on an objective, write it down. Don't limit your goals to new positions. Yes, you might set your sights on a managerial position, but other legitimate goals are to receive more recognition, to improve relationship building, to move into a more challenging situation, to learn new techniques or technologies, to gain international experience, to broaden or deepen expertise, to improve work-life balance, to increase compensation, to take advantage of educational benefits. The possibilities are limited only by your imagination.

A key factor in establishing realistic goals is to evaluate your aptitudes and how well they line up with the objective you are considering. This will help you channel your ambition in directions that are best suited to your natural abilities and strengths, and alternatively will help you set up intermediate goals aimed at developing the aptitudes you need to achieve any particular goal.

What happens when you are consciously selecting goals is that you become more active in finding out what qualifications are needed and more proactive at being truly prepared when the right opportunity arises. And opportunity does seem to arise, at least for those who are prepared for them. The opportunities that present themselves might not always line up perfectly with your stated intent, but the beauty of preparing for one thing is that it almost always seems to prepare you for many things. You can't always predict what will come along, and my advice is to try for everything that seems to fit your agenda, and then make the most of it.

When I say be prepared to take advantage of opportunities and go for every new chance that comes along, I am not advocating the do-whatever-it-takes approach to career advancement. Not at all. To have real long-term success that is deeply satisfying, you must never embrace the notions that something is your due and that it's okay to compromise your integrity in the interest of advancing your own cause. That is not career building. It inhibits personal development and is self-defeating in the long run (see Chapter 12, "Of Operators and Performers").

You are not going to be rewarded every time you apply for on an open position. Establish relationships and make friends in the interview process, be gracious if a decision doesn't go your way, and learn from the experience so you'll be better prepared next time.

What It Takes to Get Ahead

Now, let's get back to the question of what hiring managers are looking for beyond technical know-how. It's many things, actually, and even though no one on the planet will fully meet all of the requirements I list below, that doesn't stop us CIO types from seeking them. In part, that is because we are looking beyond what a candidate is to the candidate's potential to grow in terms of business value.

Decision-makers for the position you are interviewing for may attempt to gain some insight about some of the following characteristics, which I have organized into the four categories in bold:

1. A business perspective

Interviewers want to know whether you are oriented toward the business or toward cool technologies. They will lean toward the candidate who has both an interest in and an understanding of how the business acquires its customers and keeps them, an awareness of critical success factors and what role IT plays in them, and a disposition to continuously avoid cost, improve service and increase revenue with the ever more effective use of IT. Without that perspective, your interest in cool technology is out of step with the business's needs.

Ability to be comfortable at all business levels

Are you candid and friendly? Do you show a willingness to share and exchange knowledge at all levels? Can you convey that you thoroughly understand business management challenges? Can you provide examples of business goals or tasks you've had, the activities you undertook and the results you've achieved?

Strategic orientation

For some positions, interviewers will want to know whether you can look beyond business value (as important as that is) to such matters as positioning the enterprise for industry leadership, achieving operational excellence and improving business intelligence and customer intimacy, and whether you have the disposition to initiate exploratory strategic discussions around emerging technologies.

An awareness of technological trends

More than technical competence, what is being sought here is someone who knows enough about current technologies to estimate their life cycles, who can identify which emerging technologies should be watched and explain why, and who can outline some of the likely next new things in business terms.

Ability to measure and improve IT service quality

What's wanted is a person who knows practical and proven

ways to do this, who has experience in making it happen and who is able to describe how a form of continuous improvement should be implemented.

2. Success in challenging situations

Can you describe difficult events from your past career with objectivity? Interviewers aren't necessarily interested in hearing about an unending string of successes; be open about failures, while emphasizing the lessons learned. Also of interest will be how you went about recognizing any special contributions from team members who helped you through a tough time.

Superb communication skills

This one is likely to be sought no matter what position is at stake. Communication of all forms (written, spoken, in presentation) will be evaluated, so you need to be able to demonstrate these skills on your résumé, in your cover letter and, of course, during the interview itself. The reason this skill is given so much weight is that IT must be a proactive partner, not a reactive bystander, to the business. Here's a clue for you: The effective IT communicator does not use the jargon of IT. Speak the language of the business.

Proven leadership capability

This is characterized by vision, exemplary standards of behavior, the ability to inspire others, experience in introducing change, a track record of being entrusted with complex tasks of wide scope, the facility of being at ease handling broad responsibility areas, the knack for achieving stellar team performance (despite that the unplanned always happens) and a willingness to share credit, among other things. Are you someone to trust with significant enterprise resources?

Proven ability to introduce beneficial change
Here, employment decision-makers will want to know how
collaboration, persuasion and communication were used to
gain buy-in for change, what conditions or circumstances
were improved and how the results were quantified (especially when dealing with time-sensitive or critical situations).

3. Long-standing professional relationships
Do you show interest in your colleagues, the people on your
team and the people you report to? Do you demonstrate that
you care about their well-being, even taking the time to help
improve it? Do you stay in contact with people you once
worked closely with? Do you have a pattern of exchanging
help and guidance with such people? Are your relationships—in the IT profession, in the broader business world
and in the vendor community—constructive and positive?
Hiring managers will want to know these things so they can
weed out those who are poor at relationship building.

Excellent three-way and client references
Employers increasingly want to see how candidates are perceived by those who have worked for them or alongside them
and by those who have supervised them.

4. Work-life balance
Believe it or not, the person who is consumed by career will
be passed over in favor of the one who is more balanced. That
is because it is now generally recognized that steadily productive and innovative contributors take care of themselves,
their family and their professional needs in proper propor-
tion. They demonstrate personal development. They also establish exemplary standards of behavior as a kind of team
value proposition.

Willingness to relocate

This is a question that wasn't asked in days of yore, when the assumption was that all the candidates were heads of household whose careers came above all else. So today, the question becomes, "If it were right for you, your family and your work-life balance, would you consider relocating?" If it can work for you and your family situation, you might want to welcome this idea. Relocation was very beneficial for all concerned in the course of my career. The same thing applies to travel.

A record of steadily making career-building moves

This means having career direction in mind and a record of progress in that regard.

Knowledge of your own value proposition . . .

. . . and the ability to express it simply; for example: "I have a significant aptitude for optimizing processes and integrating technology solutions from a business perspective." Of course, you have to be able to back up such statements with examples.

What Else Could You Possibly Need?

Just this: Believe in yourself. If you have well-grounded faith in your qualifications and ability to meet the challenge before you, chances are you will be unanimously chosen over an otherwise identically qualified candidate. Employers know this quality when they encounter it, and they value it highly enough that it can make up for otherwise less-than-perfect qualifications. Why? Because nothing turns out exactly as planned. When surprises crop up, employers know, the best results are going to come about when they have put someone with self-belief in charge of the challenge.

You have it. Let it come through.

Index

About the Author

AL KUEBLER began his career with Computer Sciences Corporation (CSC) in assignments for the U.S. Army, the Canadian Ministry of Defense, the Marshall Space Flight Center, the U.K. Data Processing Service and others. He eventually directed all CSC Europe consulting and project operations.

He was chief information officer (CIO) for Alcatel-Lucent, Los Angeles County, AT&T Universal Card and McGraw-Hill, and director of process engineering for Citibank's Global Credit Card Division. Today, he is principal at Technical Impact, a consulting firm he founded for IT and business technology management issues.

Kuebler is a requested speaker at the graduate management schools of NYU, University of Chicago and DePaul University on the subject "Effective Information Technology: How to Get It and Keep It."

He is also a regular contributing author to *CIO* magazine, *Computerworld, Forbes* and other IT management publications.

For more information, visit *www.technicalimpact.com.* You may contact Al at ak@technicalimpact.com.

Made in the USA
Lexington, KY
23 August 2014